NEXT TIME
I FALL IN LOVE

**How To Handle Sex, Intimacy, and Feelings
in Dating Relationships**

Chap Clark

A DIVISION OF CTi
CampusLife *BOOKS* / Zondervan Publishing House
Grand Rapids, Michigan

Next Time I Fall in Love
How to Handle Sex, Intimacy, and Feelings
in Dating Relationships
Copyright © 1987 by Youth Specialties, Inc.
1224 Greenfield Drive, El Cajon, California 92021
All rights reserved

Published in cooperation with Campus Life Books, a division of CTi, and Zondervan Publishing House
Zondervan Publishing House
Grand Rapids, Michigan 49530

Library of Congress Cataloging-in-Publication Data

ISBN 0-310-58001-3

Clark, Chap, 1954.
    Next tim I fall in love / Chap Clark
        p.   cm.
    Includes bibliographical references
    Summary: Explores the concepts of friendship and love
from a Christian viewpoint and prescribes ways to have more
fullfilling dating relationships.
    ISBN 0-310-58001-3 (pbk.)
    1. Dating (Social customs)—Juvenile literature 2. Interpersonal relations—Juvenile literature. 3. Dating (Social customs)—Religious aspects—Christianity—Juvenile literature.
4. Love—Juvenile literature. [1. Dating (Social Customs) 2.
Interpersonal relations. 3. Love. 4. Christian life.]
    I. Title.
    [HQ801.C55   1990
    646.7'7—dc20   90−45019
                                                     CIP
                                                     AC

All New Testament references reprinted with permission of
MacMillan Publishing Company from *The New Testament in
Modern English* , Revised Edition, by J.B. Phillips. Copyright ©
J.B. Phillips, 1958, 1960, 1972.

Edited by Tim McLaughlin
Cover design by Dave Adamson

Printed in the United States of America

93 94 95 96 97 / CH / 9 8 7 6 5

CONTENTS

ACKNOWLEDGEMENTS

This book began as an hour-long seminar designed to help high schoolers understand the many aspects of dating relationships. Most everything else I'd heard or read on the subject of dating focused so much on "How far is too far?" and "biblical sexual standards" that most students I knew and worked with still had a hard time understanding what makes a good relationship. That was the beginning.

After two or three years of sharing some of this material at several Young Life Camps, a teacher at Rolling Hills High School asked me to come in and make a presentation to his health and driver's ed classes. As a result, I was able to teach this material for over five years in several different school settings.

The more I studied and spoke on dating, intimacy, and sex, the more I realized that most young people today, from junior highers to single adults, desperately need to understand how to develop and maintain healthy relationships.

So to all of you over the years who have taught me, affirmed me in my research and speaking, and encouraged me to press on to get some of this material out to others, I am deeply indebted:

Jim "Brownie" Brown, who told me in 1983 that he wished "every kid in the country could hear this."

Our Thursday night care group in Palos Verdes, who loved and prayed me all the way through this project.

Mike Yaconelli and Todd Temple, brothers who

have believed in me from the start.

Kathy Mulhern, who typed the manuscript in order to be the first one to read it.

The students of Glendale, Rolling Hills, and Cherry Creek High Schools, who have convinced me that God has called Dee and me to work with kids.

Jim Shelton and the rest of the Young Life staff who led me to Christ and gave me the tools and the vision to make a difference in the adolescent world.

Dee, Chappie, and Robbie, who have proven that love is not based on performance, but on commitment.

PREFACE

One warm, cloudless afternoon a few years ago I took a walk on the beach with one of the guys from the nearby high school. He and I had become good friends over the past year. We'd had many such walks, talking about everything from soccer to friends to Christ. Today, however, he was in an especially serious mood. He wanted to talk about love.

Jeff had been dating Ann for only a month. Ann had recently told him that she loved him and that, because they were now in love, they should start having sex regularly. Jeff had never been even close to experiencing anything like this before, and he was confused. He asked his father about this. His advice was, "If she wants it, go for it." So Jeff had been sleeping with Ann every day for the last week.

Sometimes he felt so good about Ann, but at other times she was moody and distant. She was jealous of his friends and wanted every free hour he had. Jeff could feel himself becoming more and more dependent on her, especially so because he had slowly cut himself off from his friends. But that was okay—he was in love.

Yesterday things had begun to change. Ann seemed bored with Jeff. She avoided him, and even walked away in the middle of a conversation. Jeff was crushed. What had gone wrong? What had he done? So he went over to her house that night to patch things up. At first Ann was distant, but then they kissed and made up. One thing led to another, and

Jeff eventually left her house filled with love and contentment.

Yet today Ann was again avoiding him. He had just fought with her earlier that afternoon. She had told him it was over, that she didn't love him anymore, and that she wanted to date another guy. With tears in his eyes, on that balmy, beautiful day at the beach, Jeff looked at me and pleaded, "She said she loved me! I thought love was supposed to last. How can something that was so right become so wrong?"

I had a hard time answering Jeff. I've seen hundreds of students, from junior high through college (and older), go through the same type of experience: a relationship that begins with fun, friendship, and romance—only to die shortly thereafter, causing pain and bitterness. How could I cut my way through this hurt and betrayal Jeff felt and help him see what went wrong?

I've written this book to help all the Anns and Jeffs to stop hurting each other in selfish relationships. God has given us a glimpse of heaven by allowing us to relate to each other, and especially by giving us the gift of loving and being loved. There is no more powerful force in human experience than the power of relationships. Once we learn the art of friendship and of love—the kind of love that gathers and sticks around when it gets tough—then we'll begin to understand what Jesus Christ wants to do and be for us.

May this book help you be a lover and a giver to those around you.

CHAPTER 1

Looking for Love

Nearly every high schooler struggles when it comes to the opposite sex. We all identify with Delia Ephron's list of worries in her book *Teenage Romance: Or, How To Die of Embarrassment*:

Worry that your breath smells.

Worry that you have B.O.

Worry that there's a right way to dress and you don't know it.

Worry that there's a right way to neck and you don't know it.

Worry that your date will be able to tell that you don't know it.

Worry that in a long kiss, you'll have to breathe through your nose and your nose will be stopped up.

Worry that, while making out, you ought to be talking, too, murmuring encouraging things like, "Oh, baby!"[1]

Worrying about love, dating, and romance takes up a lot of time and energy in high school. Perhaps the most thought-about question in the heads of 13-to-25-year-olds is, "How can I find that guy (or girl) of my dreams? Will they like me for who I am, or do I have to change? Am I too short? Too tall? Do I say the right things so people will like me and want to listen to me? Should I get aggressive and go after every person I like, or should I just sit back and be strategically shy, waiting for that special one to notice me and make the first move?"

Till Our Lips Fall Off

In the sixth grade I was in true love—LUV, we called it then—with Gail. She was fun and wild and a terrific shortstop. When our graduation party rolled around, she and I decided we liked each other. I was elated. To celebrate, we decided to sneak off to the barn next to our school with another couple and make out, which in my day simply meant kissing until your lips fell off. When we got to the barn, however, I got cold feet. I mean, after all, I had never really kissed anyone before—anyone, that is, except for my mom and dad, and occasionally my two sisters—and I wasn't too sure about this whole thing. As it turned out, the other guy's girlfriend was also too scared to go through with it, so we just sat down in the hay and watched for 45 minutes as my friend Greg and my girlfriend Gail kissed and kissed until they couldn't work their lips enough to speak. I remember thinking, "That does look like a lot of fun—but it sure looks weird!"

My curiosity and biological drives and desires took over after that, pushing me to think constantly about girls, dating, and romance. During my teenage years I can remember being interested at various times in sports, music, drama, Young Life, church—and even some classes. Yet those interests paled next to my desire to have a girlfriend—and, when I had one, to have the relationship be continually better, deeper, and more meaningful. As much as I loved playing basketball, my desire for the game was not even on the same chart as my desire for girls.

Having been around junior-high, high-school, and college students, I've concluded that my feelings, drives, and desires were not unique. A preoccupation with love, sex, and romance during the teen years is common for just about everyone. It wasn't just us guys on my high-school basketball team who took that one last look in the mirror before running out onto the court. Nearly every guy does that. Why? To intimidate the other team? Hardly. They know there are girls in those stands.

Sorting Through the Garbage

But why is it that, with these urges and desires — these deep feelings in everyone's bodies during their teenage years — authentic answers and explanations are so hard to get, *except* from our records, TV shows, and movies? Do we really learn what love is by watching *Love Boat* reruns or listening to Madonna sing to us about how good sex was "the very first time"? Some young people are fortunate enough to know a few adults who know enough and care enough to help sort out the truth from the garbage, the healthy from the destructive — maybe a minister, a teacher, a Young Life or Campus Life leader, or a parent. But most are on their own to figure out how to deal with the opposite sex and how to develop some guidelines that will lead to happiness instead of heartache.

I hope this book will help give you a good shot at forming and keeping healthy relationships. This is not a book about merely setting sexual moral standards; or understanding your sexual needs, drives, and desires; or even choosing the right partner — though we'll touch on each of these. What this book

is about is answering these questions:
- What's the nature of love?
- What's the difference between falling in love and choosing to be in love?
- What can hurt a relationship? What can heal a relationship or improve it?

Even as we start talking about dating, I know that an army of subtle fears begins creeping up. "Who'd want to date me? What about my looks? I don't have enough money to date, and I don't know how to talk to girls (or guys), and let's face it—I'm just plain too scared to go on a real date."

The whole concept of dating has changed drastically over the past several years. It's pretty rare these days for a guy to call a girl he hardly knows and ask her to go out with him. Most of what we call dating today is almost any kind of group doing something together socially. Virtually no one talks about "dating" someone. It's far more common to be "going out" with that special someone.

So in this book we won't be talking much about a typical dating relationship. Instead we'll concentrate on how any two people who care for each other can make the best of the institution of "going out."

If you're 13 to 25 years old, or if you know anyone that age, and if you're interested in learning more about how to be happy, healthy, and whole in a dating relationship—then these pages will help you.

In a word . . .

Understanding dating relationships isn't easy for anyone. We all could use older friends who can help us learn how to cultivate them.

Ask yourself—

1. What scares you most about the opposite sex?
2. If there was one thing you could ask about dating, what would it be? Why?

CHAPTER 2

I Love Green Beans!

I love my mom and dad.
I love my dog.
I love football.
I love Sadie Glucksmeyer, my girlfriend.
I love green beans.

Love. The word is so versatile for us. It means anything from a warm, tender feeling for a new boyfriend or girlfriend to a self-indulgence for a favorite food. No wonder it's so hard for us to know when we are in love.

Love describes a variety of feelings.

Since the word is so difficult to pin down, how can we distinguish being in love from mere infatuation, or from a desire just to get to know someone? If we want healthy, growing, and honest relationships, we must first figure out that strange word *love*.

But this is tougher than it looks. Who's to say what love really is? After all, the word has as many uses as there are people. Our best course, perhaps, is to glance back over our shoulders into the past—specifically, back to the ancient Greeks—for they had a lot to say about love.

The Greeks were into love. In fact, they had five different words for it. Two of them, *eros* (pronounced

EH-ross) and *agape* (ah-GAW-pay), may help us understand our own word *love*.

Eros to Erotic to Adult Bookstores

When you see *eros* on the page, what English word comes to mind? *Erotic*, of course! And then what? Mud-wrestling, X-rated movies—raw sex.

During my college days, students would pay money to sit on a hard gym floor for the annual Erotic Film Festival—12 hours of triple-X films, one after another. When they returned, they carried a subtle, sickly guilt.

"Did you have fun?" I asked some friends of mine who had gone.

"Well, kind of, but . . . well, no—not really."

"Then why did you go, or why didn't you leave once you saw what it was?"

"I dunno. I guess it was supposed to be really neat, all those hyper-sexy scenes and all. But it . . . well, it just seemed so empty. I kind of wish I hadn't gone. Those guys make sex seem kind of cheap and dirty."

Erotic bookstores abound in big cities. Erotic magazines sell like hotcakes around the world. Sell what? Just what the English word *erotic* indicates—sex. Raw, selfish, simple, lonely sex. Derived from the valuable Greek word *eros*, the English word *erotic* has come to be synonymous with a no-strings-attached, fun-and-games sexual lifestyle.

The Greek word *eros* was more lofty than the English word *erotic* with its purely sexual definition. *Eros* was originally and simply a passionate love for a thing. In this original sense, then, *eros* may be love of cats, or of *Cats*; love of football—whether as player or spectator—or of skiing; love of most anything. As long as it's a passionate love.

But isn't such a passionate love wrong or sinful? Of course not. God Himself created beauty and wants us to admire and appreciate whoever and whatever is marked by it. Even to the Greeks there was no moral wrong associated with the word *eros*. An Eros love is a good and noble thing.

Even sexual passion, including the romantic feelings and desires we all have, are often referred to as erotic. God doesn't draw a line forbidding the fun and excitement of sexual passion. Neither is he displeased with our powerful sexual longings. To the contrary, God has created us to experience life in its fullness and to know him and enjoy his creation. Sexual pleasure and passion—erotic love—is a gift from the hand of God.

Like most gifts he gives us, however, the love and enjoyment of sexual pleasure can be used for giving, as he intended, or used selfishly. And to complicate things, the sweeter and more powerful a gift is, the more potential it has for disaster. The passion that is Eros is a fantastic, tender, and beautiful gift—when it's placed within the context of a committed love relationship. Used selfishly, Eros is devastating in its power to destroy people and relationships.

Veggie Passion

In order to get a better picture of Eros and to understand a modern Eros relationship, I'll let you in on a family secret—I have an Eros relationship with green beans. Honest. I crave them, yearn for them, long for them.

When I told my wife Dee that I loved green beans, she made me green beans—mounds of them—twice a week for months. Ah, their aroma, their taste—I couldn't get enough.

But soon I began to like them less and less. Slowly but surely I began getting a bit nauseous every time I got a whiff of them cooking. Yet I wouldn't admit it to myself—I loved them so! One day, however, I walked into the kitchen, and there on the stove was a fresh batch of green beans just waiting for me to pounce on them, fork in hand. I finally cracked.

"Throw them out! Get rid of every last green bean!"

"Why?" Dee asked. "Something wrong with these green beans?"

"It's not *those* green beans; it's *all* green beans. I just looked in the mirror—I'm turning green! I'm starting to *look* like a green bean! Aagghh!"

What had delighted me now repulsed me. I discovered that Eros is *temporary*.

You know it, too. You look forward to Thanksgiving—no school, football, rest, family, and food. Especially turkey. Everyone loves turkey, some with a passionate, Eros love. So on Thursday you stuff yourself with turkey. That night you munch on turkey sandwiches and more pie. The next morning your visiting aunt whips up turkey omelets. By the end of Thanksgiving vacation—and after four days of turkey soup, turkey sandwiches, turkey salad, and turkey ice cream—you never want to see another turkey again. You even have second thoughts about the Pilgrims.

Why does this happen? Because an Eros love relationship is love for an object, it's easy for us to misuse or abuse the thing or activity that we love. I love passionately—until, that is, I grow tired or bored of my beloved, whether my beloved is green beans or turkey or a person. Eros lasts only as long as I want it to last. When Eros is gone, I'm ready to check out of the relationship and move on to other loves that give me new pleasures.

. . . *With Anchovies — But Hold the Beans*

There's more to Eros. Plopped in front of the TV with a few friends watching a football game, we were just beginning to devour a fresh anchovy pizza when Dee popped into the room with a steaming bowl of green beans. (This was before I gave them up.) I loved green beans — but not with pizza. My love for green beans had, for the moment, been replaced by my love for anchovy pizza.

Dee thought she was doing me a favor by bringing me my favorite food for lunch. My response wasn't as gracious.

"Yuck. I can't stand the smell of those green beans."

"But I thought you loved green beans!"

"I did — last night with a roast and potatoes. But with anchovy pizza, I don't want to even see a green bean."

Now it was curious that, although my friends let me have it for treating my wife the way I did, none of them scolded me for mistreating the green beans. Nobody rebuked me; no one told me, "What a jerk! How could you treat those poor beans like that? Last night you told them you loved them, and today you ignore them."

I can treat them like that because Eros is *conditional*. When you love with Eros, you will love so long as the beloved meets specific conditions — and when those conditions are no longer fulfilled, you withdraw your love. "I love you passionately, green beans — but only

21

if you're cooked just right and served with the proper meal and . . . "

Me, Myself, and I

One more trait of Eros. The sort of love I have for green beans is gratified only when I taste them. Bubbling in the saucepan or piled in the serving bowl, they only tease my desire to eat them. The whole point of loving green beans with Eros love is tasting them, and that usually means boiling, grinding, and swallowing them—in other words, to love green beans is to destroy them, or at least use them for my own gratification.

In other words, Eros is *self-centered*. It's a relationship that's centered around and focused on me. Eros is a for-me love. I'm committed to the welfare of my beloved only if it benefits me. What happens to those green beans is not really my ultimate concern. My ultimate concern is getting my own satisfaction and pleasure out of what I love.

Eros, then, is temporary, conditional, and self-centered. Most times we say we love this or that thing, chances are we mean Eros. If we listen closely to ourselves, in fact, we'll probably discover that Eros is simply a love for ourselves. It's not really love for something outside ourselves at all. Eros is self-love. "I want what's best for me," Eros asserts. "When this thing that now brings me pleasure pleases me no longer, I will abandon it."

Now let's look at another way altogether of loving.

In a word . . .

The word *love* has many uses for us today. One popular use is what the Greeks called *eros*—a temporary, conditional, self-centered love for a person or thing or activity.

Ask yourself—

1. List the ways you use the word *love*. How many of those can be considered Eros-type loves?
2. Is it wrong to love something with Eros? Why or why not?
3. Is a passionate love for an object (Eros) *always* temporary, conditional, and self-centered? What are some reasons for your conclusions?

CHAPTER 3

Agape Love: John and Sue

In the fall of his junior year, my best friend John first noticed a cute, quiet girl in our class. Sue was shy and obviously spent little time around wild types like John and me. But one night at a football victory party, Sue ended up sitting on the couch next to John.

The more they talked, the more John realized that he liked getting to know Sue. He didn't have a crush on her, but just plain liked her. So that night at the party, John asked Sue out. A week or two later John and Sue were officially "going out."

Now when most couples get official, they begin the long, slow process of shutting off all their old friends, of getting wrapped up in themselves, of expecting more and more from each other, of succumbing to the pressures of heavy sexual involvement, of gradually smothering each other—in a word, killing what could be a fun relationship.

John and Sue wanted to be different. They wanted a relationship that was both fun and right, and so they made some decisions that they felt would give them a better shot at a healthy relationship. Together they chose three things to work on: first, to not let their relationship interfere with any of their other friendships. Second, they made a pact to work hard at controlling their physical relationship. And third, they committed themselves to being honest and open with each other.

And were they ever different! Sure, they had their fights and tough times like any couple. But they also had a depth and strength in their relationship that the whole school noticed. They also had that rare something that every couple wants but few attain—happiness. They were happy together, and no less happy apart. And a year and a half later, when they decided it was time to move on, John and Sue were able to remain close friends who deeply cared for each other.

This is the type of relationship that wants the best for it and is willing to do whatever it takes to make it last. John and Sue's relationship is a far cry from Eros—love for a thing—that was discussed in the last chapter. John and Sue's love was something else altogether.

Giving, Committed, Lasting

It's called Agape. You've probably heard of it before, since it's used so much in the New Testament. Writers of Scripture used it to describe the kind of love God has for us, his people. Agape, says one Greek dictionary, is "an unselfish love, ready to serve."[1] Agape is the sort of love that says that *your* needs, *your* wants, *your* desires are more important than mine—a for-you kind of love. Agape means that I'm in the relationship for what I can *give* to the other person, not for what I can get. Agape love is, in other words, *giving*.

Agape is not only giving, but committed. The Greek dictionary adds that Agape is a "deliberate choice" rather than a helpless falling in love.[2] Agape says that when I decide to love someone, I make a conscious choice to care for her. So when I claim to love with an Agape love, that means I'm committing myself to my partner.

And Agape lasts. It is "not an impulse from the feelings; it does not always run with the natural inclinations,"our Greek dictionary again tells us.[3] So much is made of—how do they say it?—"being in love." "Our relationship has gone sour," oodles of people have told me, because they were no longer "in love" or that "the love's gone out" of their relationship—as if love is a separate entity that comes and goes as it pleases.

That's a scary thought. Let's say you're married, or even just dating. You really love that special person. You're pretty lucky, you think, to find comfort and security in your relationship. Then one day, *boom*— "Thanks for the memories," you're told, "but I don't feel anything for you anymore, so I guess I don't love you. See ya," and out they walk, out the door, out of your life.

But what was it that you had, if it was so fragile that it could fall apart just like that? If you can fall out of love so easily, how can you trust another enough to be open and intimate with them? Face it—we fall in and out of love so quickly and effortlessly that it's surprising we ever trust anyone with our hearts.

But Agape—consistent, healthy, human love—is one continual decision; it's choosing to love even if fickle emotions insist that love has flown. If two people are committed to each another in an Agape love, their love is never gone. It is just an ember lying low, waiting for a little romance to fan it into flame. Like God himself, Agape never leaves us; it simply may be lying dormant, obscured by the cloudiness of the daily routine.

What works for dating works for marriage — it's still Agape that cultivates an exciting, healthy marriage. In fact, these same principles of love apply to all relationships. But right now we're talking about developing and maintaining *dating* relationships that, for most, will never lead to marriage. So where does Agape, a committed and chosen love, fit for high-school students more interested in a fun date than in a wedding?

"All I Want's a Date, Not a Husband!"

The answer lies in the degree of commitment in a relationship. The amount of Agape — that is, the kind of love that is *decided on* and not *fallen into* — is the only accurate measuring stick of how much for-you love there is in a relationship. Now I realize that a young dating couple can be committed to each other only so far. A high schooler's Agape, for example, will probably amount to much less than a seriously dating college couple's. But that for-you love, regardless of its amount, is still the only accurate gauge of how healthy the relationship is. The only reliable love is one promised by choice rather than propelled by emotion.

Look at the relationship of John and Sue. There was little question in either's mind that they liked each other. So when they set limits on their dating life, they had nothing to fear — they weren't nervous about losing a shaky love, nor doubting their relationship when they were apart, nor jealous when around other friends. They trusted each other because their love was a committed, Agape love. They knew that it was a healthy relationship characterized by a spirit of giving and commitment, and that therefore it would last.

If you are in a dating relationship, ask yourself how yours looks when compared with John and Sue's. Are you involved because you've chosen to be together as friends? Or are you together because of convenience, of fear, or of what you can get out of the relationship? Maybe there's a romantic pull, but little else. Without a deliberate choice of care and commitment, even the most powerful romantic feelings have a hard time fueling a relationship. You can trust love's feelings to survive no longer than a song survives on the charts. Such love is great for a while, but you can't trust it to be around forever.

Romance, emotional urges, and physical attraction are all exciting—but without a deliberately chosen, two-way, Agape, for-you foundation, the relationship is doomed. And though total commitment is not necessary, you'll need some degree of commitment if you want a healthy relationship.

In a word . . .

True love is best described by the Greek concept behind the word Agape, which is giving, committed, and lasting love.

Ask yourself—

1. What was good about John and Sue's relationship? What wasn't so good?
2. Can you "fall into" Agape love? Why or why not?
3. How can Agape love still be there after a break-up?

CHAPTER 4

Dating:
Eros or Agape?

Love, then, can come in two varieties—Eros (a for-me love for an object or thing) and Agape (a for-you, committed love for a person). And when you put them next to each other, do they ever look different!

Lasting vs. Temporary

Eros is temporary; Agape, lasting. Eros says, "When I lose interest in you, when I've used you, when I don't need you any more, we're through with each other." Agape says, "Time will strengthen my love and care for you, making it better, stronger, sweeter." Agape vows to the beloved, "Because you are unique, special, and valuable, I will always be your friend. I'm not in this just for myself—I'm mainly interested in you. And that means you can count on me to be here tomorrow."

Agape lovers never tire of their partners. Now as the dating relationship deepens, you may sense that it's not the best or even what you really want. But that's not necessarily getting tired of the person. It's rather a need to move on to other relationships because you know this isn't the best one for you. And if it's not best for you, then neither is it best for your partner.

So as the time comes to move on, Agape keeps communication between partners open and honest. Though it may be hard to remain friendly and frank and gentle when your relationship has outgrown its commitment, it will still be the most caring thing you can do for your friend. For Agape is sensitive even at the end of a relationship. When a dating partnership shifts down to a friendship, there should be few surprises. Care, gentleness, and honesty remain the trademarks of Agape—while selfishness, fear, hurt, and confusion characterize Eros.

Conditional vs. Committed

Eros is also characterized by its conditional nature. Agape, remember, is a committed love. Eros, on the other hand, loves only when certain conditions are met—one wrong step and it's all over. An Agape relationship is committed to the other person without conditions. "No matter what you say, how you behave, who you hang around with, or even how you treat me, I will love you for life," the Agape lover says.

An Eros relationship offers little real security—the relationship always hangs by a thread. Because it's based on performance, looks, or chemistry, you've got to be on your guard to make sure you're always pleasing your partner by how you look, speak, and act. You know that in an Eros relationship keeping your boyfriend or girlfriend may be a delicate matter of constantly having to please them. That inevitably causes you to say things you don't mean and do things you don't want to do.

In an Agape relationship you can rest and relax knowing that you can be yourself without fear of losing your boyfriend or girlfriend by being foolish or boring. You are loved and cared for because of *who* you are, not *what* you are.

Agape showers a relationship with necessary freedom. There's seldom any doubt that the love you receive springs from a desire to know and care for you as a person. It's truly a for-you relationship that stresses the other's needs and desires above your own. As both of you love with Agape, with no strings attached, both are surprisingly well cared for and happy in the relationship.

However happy they may *think* they are, those in Eros relationships constantly live with a secret fear of losing what they are working so hard to keep. In the end there's little lasting happiness for anyone in an Eros, for-me relationship.

Self-centered vs. Giving

Finally, Eros and Agape differ in that Eros is purely self-centered. It declares, "I am involved with you because of what it can be for me." Which is why an Eros relationship is a for-me relationship.

At the very core of Agape, on the other hand, is giving. When I say that I love someone (Agape), I am more concerned with what I can give to the relationship and to the other person than I am about what I can get. An Agape love is best described as a for-you relationship.

See the contrast? Eros in itself is not a bad thing— Eros is part of us, part of what God created. But a dating relationship based on Eros is usually a dead-end street.

As foolish as it seems to try to find joy and fulfillment in an Eros relationship, the majority of students

I've known over the years tell me that nearly every dating relationship they've seen leans more toward Eros than Agape—80 to 90 percent, they claim. My own experience with kids in Young Life confirms this. If people want more and deserve better than selfish and painful relationships, why do most of them surrender again and again to no-win Eros?

Love Is a Mixed Bag

Part of the problem is the difficulty in drawing a solid line between a healthy and an unhealthy relationship. When two people come together as dating partners, there's always going to be a mixture of healthy and unhealthy aspects. Every relationship has some Eros and some Agape in it.

Let's face it—we're all selfish to some extent. We all have our moments of being overly needy or hypersensitive. Yet Agape sounds so lofty, so unattainable, that when we look at how we really are, we see why we fall so short of the ideal. We can try and try, but we'll never be able to love with the purity of Agape love.

So even the best dating friendship will fall somewhere between these two loves. In order to maintain a happy and fulfilling dating relationship, however, it needs at least to be tipped toward the Agape end.

Eros Relationship ———— Agape Relationship

In a word . . .

Eros (love for a thing) and Agape (love for a person) represent opposites in a relationship. All dating relationships fall somewhere between these two ways of relating to people. This book can help you get closer to Agape love in your relationships.

Ask yourself—

1. In your own setting—school, dorm, etc.—what percentage of dating relationships that you know of lean toward Eros? Agape? Why do you think they do?
2. Is it possible to have an Eros relationship that's fun? That's healthy? Why or why not?
3. If you could choose, would you rather be involved in an Eros or an Agape relationship? Why?

CHAPTER 5

Self-Esteem: "Why Would Anyone Want To Date Me?"

Cruising the aisles of a hardware store one week-end on a errand trip with my five-year-old son, I heard a high pitched scream from another part of the store.

"DAAADDY–quick! Come see this!"

Realizing there was only one set of lungs that could make that much noise, I ran to the back, prepared to unleash some righteous parental anger on the boy. But when I turned the corner of the aisle, I saw a two-foot tall, 345-pound five-year-old. And then I saw my son posing in front of a warped mirror, something like what you see at carnivals. He was delighted with the distortion.

What if that warped mirror was the only mirror in your house? You'd see only a short, fat pudgkins. Out on the street you'd envy all those tall, lithe people legging their graceful way here and there. What a complex you'd have! Fat you. Dumb you. The problem, of course, would be the quality of the mirror hanging on your wall, not yourself.

Absurd, I know. We know what we really look like because we know what mirrors to trust. But what about the *inner* you? What mirrors do you have to reveal what you're like on the inside? How do you measure your inner self-image? Let's go a step further — how do images of the real, inner you affect how you relate to others? Let's look at three different mirrors most of us peer into to figure out how we look on the inside.

Jumping Through Society's Hoops

We've grown up in a culture that demands success. It's a subtle yet powerful current that tugs at us, that tells us that in order to succeed in life, we have to measure up to society's standards. The pressure to look good, get good grades, make the right friends, join the right teams, be seen at the right parties — these pressures force many teenagers to value themselves according to their performance.

What girl hasn't grown up half believing that only the pretty and popular girls deserve attention and affection? The cosmetic and fashion industries hold up an especially warped mirror for girls to view themselves in. They spend billions of dollars to convince girls that they're not as pretty and glamorous as they could be. Advertisers are expert at making consumers think they need, must have, can't live without their products. So most women believe they need to buy something to make themselves more attractive. They believe the myth that something must be wrong with them if they're not beautiful. Subscribe to *Mademoiselle*, one TV commercial urges, and "experience the make-up tips that *right nature's wrongs*."

High schools hold up mirrors that are just as

warped. Homecoming and prom-queen elections simply reinforce society's reminder to young women: "God really messed up when he made you." Few schools even bother pretending that their cheerleader tryouts are based on skill and ability. Everyone, including the girls, knows that good looks and sex appeal go farther in snagging a spot on the varsity cheer squad. Ever talk to girls who didn't make the first cut in cheerleading tryouts or prom queen contests? Not only do they not especially like themselves—they often *hate* themselves.

Teenage guys aren't exempt, either, from using distorted mirrors of society to look at themselves. Boys learn to tell early in life who's cool, who's "in"—and who's not. "Want to be cool and 'in,' guys? Then," you're told, "perform. Jump through the hoops. Be aggressive. Get what you want." The only way you'll feel good about yourself, you're told, is to grit and grind it out and do better than anyone else. Your performance is everything. Whether you want to be liked in a new neighborhood, be accepted at school, or move ahead in business, you're told that you have to be competitive at every level. And society will judge you not as you are, but as you perform. Which means if you don't win at whatever you do, you're a nobody.

And so you struggle—struggle to look just right, to perform just right to please your classmates and boyfriends and girlfriends, to fit in. You're judged, labelled, and shelved by your culture according to how well you do and how you impress others. It's a continual battle to make it in your culture and yet keep some sense of personal respect and identity.

But most people lose that battle. They wind up trusting society's mirror for how they look—and inevitably they appear in that mirror as warped and as culturally pudgy as my son did in the hardware store. They don't look like Christie Brinkley and don't play football like John Elway. They're plain, ordinary people—just average—and so they walk away from the mirror feeling like a flop, a failure. Who'd ever want to date the person in that mirror?

With Friends Like These . . .

Not only do we get our self-image from how we look and how we succeed at the world's games, but we depend also on the mirror of our friendships. Friends are often first to point out mistakes or wrong turns we've made—and that kind of criticism hurts. If we pay too much attention to their opinions of us, they turn us into something we're not. If we're honest and had to choose between being liked by our friends and being ourselves, we know what we'd probably choose.

This isn't to say that a friend who's truly loyal, who's honest with you and really likes you can't be a healthy mirror, a mirror that gives you an accurate reflection of what you're really like. But let's face it— we want so badly to be liked and considered important that it's easy to let the criticism get to us more than the encouragement. And so our self-image suffers.

The If-Only Game

Despite the warped mirrors that schools, the media, and friends hold up before you, an even worse distortion may be reflected by your own expectations. The defective mirror you hold up to yourself may twist your self-image terribly.

You may be attractive, intelligent, popular, funny, athletic—the last person to have a self-image problem. But then you look around, start comparing, and promptly fall into the If-Only game:

"If only I were cuter, then I would have more dates."

"If only I were more outgoing like Tessa . . . "

"If only I made first string like Donn, I'd *really* be in . . . "

Even statistics suggest it. One survey found that 68 percent of the polled teenagers said they liked themselves—which means that one out of three said outright that they *didn't* like themselves.[1] If you even occasionally feel unlucky or unlovely, you're not alone.

How does all this affect dating? For some, a poor self-image and consequent urgency to be liked actually drives people away. You've probably noticed how the ones who seem to need love the most have the hardest time finding it. The saddest thing is that when you enter a relationship hoping to fill your own needs, you're dooming it—because you've created from the start an Eros, for-me relationship. As long as I need to be loved in order to feel good about myself, I'm trapped—simply because I can never *give* as much love as I demand in return. I'm too busy watching out for number one.

Secure Enough Not To Date

At a football game I ran into a senior named Jill. The daughter of a famous actor, she was bright and very attractive, with an air of confidence about her. The more I got to know Jill in the following weeks, the more I began to see her as someone who was desperately hiding behind a bright and bubbly exterior. Her father had divorced her mother when she was a child—and her mom had hardly spent any time with her at all. She barely knew her dad, but liked to brag about how good he was to her. But the closer one got to Jill, the more hollow the words sounded. The fact was that Jill had such a low view of herself that she needed to accumulate people in order to get love and attention. She was starved for someone to care for her.

Once Jill saw that she had the looks and the personality to attract friends, she stopped trying to wring love and security out of her parents and began latching onto whomever gave her a semblance of attention—especially guys. They'd take her out once or twice, lured by her reputed willingness to do just about anything—but they soon fled because of the way she'd cling to them. As far as I knew, she didn't have a single real friend throughout her high-school years. There were too many strings attached for any authentic friendships to bloom. Jill needed love so desperately, was so urgently trying to be loved, that she didn't take the time or expend the energy to give love.

Only when you get a good, healthy handle on your self-image can you be freed up to enter a relationship for what you can give. Do you want a healthy relationship? It needs two independently healthy, whole people who are happy and secure without feeling like they *have* to date in order to feel good about themselves. Only when you have enough self-confidence not to need to date can you freely give love.

If you can't trust society or your friends or even yourself to tell you what you're really like inside, then who do you trust? Where can you get an accurate reflection of the real you? Is there an unwarped mirror you can view yourself in?

Of course there is. That mirror is God himself. How God sees you is how you actually, truly are.

What Does God See in You?

He sees you as one-of-a-kind, first of all. Look at your hands. Study them. Those hands are unique in the history of the universe. They are the original, just-right creations of Jesus Christ. Your voice, your toes, your eyes, your smile – all individual, all unique, all special. You're a one-of-a-kind masterpiece – a veritable work of art.

Did you hear about the nervy student tourist in a French art museum? The guide stopped before the canvas of a stunning landscape and tried to convey the genius behind such a concept, such brushwork, such artistry. The kid turned to his companion and remarked, "I don't think it's that great."

The guide overheard him. "This is a unique masterpiece of one of the greatest artists," he told the visiting student. "It has withstood the test of centuries. The painting is not on trial – you are."

Those who try to convince you that you're plain or stupid or a nobody are as arrogant as that student. The Master made you – you are a masterpiece. You're not on trial – it's the mirrors of our culture that need straightening. You are unique, exactly as your Artist designed you.

You Have Something To Give

Secondly, you're talented. We live in a diverse

world, after all. And that means, among other things, that we each have some gift or talent to give to others. Something. It may not be obvious or what the world recognizes as stupendous. But each of us has something that others need and that only we can give.

He Doesn't Care That We Stink

Not only are you unique and talented, but you're weak. Well, aren't you? Let's face it—everyone stinks in at least a few areas. But that's the beauty of it—*everyone* fails, everyone blows it. And that's okay. Just don't dwell on your failures, or else you'll drive people away. Let your shortcomings remind you where you need to improve, but don't let them persuade you that you're a flop.

The central message in the Bible is not that we're perfect by the world's standards and that's why God likes us. The message is that God loves us in spite of ourselves—is delighted with us, in fact. And because he removes our guilt as well as forgives us, you and I can move ahead, no longer paralyzed by fear and guilt.

So when you look at yourself in God's mirror—the only accurate reflection of the *real* you, free of distortion—you'll begin to see a beautiful, unique, and special creation of the great King of the universe—a King you don't have to perform for or succeed in something for. You just need to trust Him when he says he loves you. And in that perfect mirror you see someone who's unique, talented, and—like everyone else—needs improvement. Give yourself time to improve—society's done quite a job on you already, and you're not going to shake its warped reflections of you overnight.

People will constantly disappoint you, put you down, and expect of you things you can't deliver— but God will never let you down. He loves you too much.

In a word . . .

You are a unique and talented child of God who is both lovable and likeable. You are a masterpiece of the Creator, and the more you see yourself as valuable and worthy of affection, the better you'll be at succeeding in an Agape, for-you relationship.

Ask yourself—

1. Quickly now—list five things you like about yourself. List five things you dislike about yourself. Which was easier? Why?
2. What are some things about yourself you want to thank God for? List them and thank Him.
3. How does a healthy self-image affect dating?

CHAPTER 6

Feelings: Dating's Roller Coaster

The first day in my first class of my sophomore year in high school, I saw her—the prettiest girl I had ever seen (or so I felt at the time). Every girl I had ever liked seemed to be molded into this vision of beauty before me. For months I couldn't get Sharon off my mind. I was convinced I was in love with her.

Has that ever happened to you?

The funny thing was that as much as I was hooked on her, I had no idea what she was like. In fact, if anyone had asked me about her, all I could have described were my feelings for her and my desire to date her. She was a virtual stranger; we hung around different groups; our paths never crossed—and yet I thought I was in love. Because I hung on stubbornly to my secret love, it was a long time before I grew out of this crush.

You won't have any trouble recognizing Eros love in this sophomore fling of mine. I wasn't interested in her, but in a portrait, a walking statue, a symbol, a shadow of some ideal woman I had created. Sharon and I eventually became friends, but my early infatuation with her had nothing to do with who she was. I merely projected into her my own desire for a certain kind of girl with a certain appearance. Something about Sharon—her smile, the way she walked, how she did her hair—pressed some button deep inside me that aroused strong feelings of love in me. But it wasn't the person Sharon that did this—only her appearance.

What a mess I would have made of things if she had liked me. I had no desire to truly like her and enjoy her for who she was inside as a person. I would have treated her like just a pretty face. I would have put her on display and expected her to live up to my idea of what she should be like. Instead of caring for her, I would have been caring for myself.

Short-lived and Superficial

It's called infatuation. The dictionary calls it "foolish love or affection." In *Handling Your Hormones: The Straight Scoop on Love and Sexuality*, author Jim Burns calls the feeling I had for Sharon a "short-lived and superficial attraction to another person."[1] Earlier in the book we've called this sort of thing Eros. Society calls it *falling in love*.

Whatever you call it, it's not real love—though it feels for the world like it is. It hits powerfully—and often: Burns claims that you'll fall in love with probably five different people between ninth grade and your second year in college. I'm convinced that he's right—I can't think of too many times during my adolescence when I *wasn't* in love with somebody.

But then how do you distinguish real love from infatuation, especially since infatuation—falling in love—*feels* so much like love? It's a crucial question, because starting out in the fantasy of falling in love and *then* turning it around into a for-you dating relationship is difficult.

Falling in love definitely exists. However faulty and dangerous Eros or infatuation may be to build a dating relationship on, you can't deny its existence. Palms sweat, noses run, and stomachs churn just at the thought of another. So what do these feelings of love mean?

Intense but Unreliable

First, feelings of falling in love contain only a piece of reality. Sure, these rich, intense, aromatic feelings of love prompt us to date people. Falling in love definitely tells us that we're excited about someone. But for all the usefulness of infatuation, it will turn on you viciously if you think those feelings are all you need for a loving relationship.

As a gauge of Agape love — a for-you love — romantic feelings simply aren't reliable, largely because they ignore the facts. *Star Trek's* Mr. Spock, for example, led a pretty impassionate existence, thanks to his Vulcan ancestry. His value to the purely human crew on the *Enterprise* lay in his ability to think with stark logic when others' emotions got in the way. Now Spock is no perfect model for humanity, but we can learn from him. It's important for us to take a close look at what we're getting excited about and to check out how much reality there is to support our feelings.

Up One Minute, Down the Next

Not only are romantic feelings an unreliable yardstick, they fluctuate like crazy. To someone in love (Eros), romantic feelings are up one day and down the next. All sorts of things inside and around you sway romantic love one way or the other—the physical changes of adolescence, normal mood swings, diet, exercise, pressure from family or friends or school. On the other hand, Agape love is not nearly as susceptible to such fluctuation. The more level and consistent the feelings over time, the healthier the relationship.

You Can't Just Turn Them Off

Thirdly, romantic feelings of love are powerful and difficult to control. Ever try to drum up romantic feelings for someone? "I *will* like her, I *will* like her, I *will* like her, I *will* . . . " It just doesn't work. Of course, we all wish we could turn our feelings on and off like a faucet. Who wouldn't rather perk themselves up when they're feeling down, or turn off feelings for people they know are terrible for them so they could just drop them cold? Feelings just have to run their course while we try not to rely on them too heavily.

If you do give romantic feelings free rein, on the other hand, you'll have a terrible time trying to control them later. If you let them, romantic feelings will overpower your common sense and even your will power. You may have decided that you absolutely don't want to become involved with someone who's into drugs or drinking, for example—but if you let yourself fall in love with someone like that, you'll compromise your decision.

No Thanks, Spock

Finally, no one can deny that romantic feelings add spice to life. Though it was Spock's cold logic that saved the *Enterprise* who-knows-how-many times, I'm glad that I'm not a Vulcan—I want to feel life. For all their shortcomings, romantic feelings are among the most exciting, fun, and stimulating of all the emotions. Rolled up in romance is a potent mix of fear and joy and anticipation and excitement and adventure. I wouldn't trade romantic love for anything— even though most of my life it's driven me crazy.

"But What Do I Do With My Feelings?"

As exciting as they are, how can we trust our feelings if they're so unreliable, or keep them in check if they're so uncontrollable?

Know them for what they are, first of all. Welcome romantic feelings as part of the dating adventure— but don't read into them any more than they deserve. Just because you're wild about someone, don't jump to the conclusion that you've found true love. Romantic feelings don't necessarily indicate a desire to be committed; they just give us the incentive to keep on getting to know each other.

Don't trust them too much, either. Because romantic feelings and emotions fluctuate so much, it can be a mistake to make far-reaching decisions based solely on our feelings. Sure, emotions are important in love relationships—but so are commitment, friendship, honesty, loyalty, and forethought.

Yet enjoy the power and spice of romance. So far we've talked about the dangers of relying on feelings. It's just as damaging to a relationship to ignore or suppress feelings. They need to be expressed—in fact, their very nature demands that they be verbalized. Don't think that feelings are bad. They're neither bad nor good, but neutral. What they do is illuminate what we're really thinking deep inside us. So acknowledge what's inside you. Share your feelings honestly — and share them often — with someone you trust. Hiding or running from feelings never works; they'll inevitably chase us down and bite us. Express them and enjoy the adventure they bring to life.

Don't let the beauty and simplicity of falling in love destroy you and your special friends. Make sure your mind, your heart, and your commitment are a dating relationship's foundation so that when those overpowering romantic feelings surge, they can be welcomed as friends that actually improve a date instead of enemies that are out to destroy you and the friendship.

In a word . . .

About romantic feelings —
- They contain only a piece of reality.
- They constantly fluctuate.
- They're difficult to control.
- They're powerful.
- They add spice to life.

Handling these feelings —
- Know them for what they are.
- Don't trust them too much.
- Enjoy them!

Ask yourself—

1. Define *infatuation* in your own words.
2. What is the difference between being infatuated and being in love?
3. How can you learn to handle the romantic feelings of being in love?

CHAPTER 7

Time Together: The Book of Love

The most well-known textbook on today's high-school campus has never been officially distributed to students, never had assignments made from it—in fact, it's never been printed. But it's been read and studied by almost every teenager.

The name of this book? *The Rules of Dating.*

Go ahead—open it up and flip through it. Chapter One, "What To Do When Starting Off," offers pointers like "Never let people you date know what you *really* think of them" and "It's important to pretend to want to kiss on the first date—even if you don't want to—otherwise the word will get out that you're either a tease or a prude."

Here's a chapter entitled "Time Together," and it warns that "once dating, don't ever forget that you *own* each other"—which means that you must be together between every class, on the phone every night, and that both weekend nights are reserved for your boyfriend or girlfriend. Any slip in these matters is just cause for your partner to break up and move on to someone who's willing to play by *The Rules of Dating.*

Sound familiar? Do these rules resemble those in your school or among your friends? The unwritten law that requires exclusive and smothering time together in high school — and even college — seems to be enforced from L.A. to Boston, from Atlanta to Seattle. The rules that define dating relationships are remarkably similar all across the U.S. of A.

That doesn't mean that the rules haven't changed over the years. Not too long ago, for example, a girl was publicly identified with her steady by wearing his ring or letterman's sweater or jacket. Now it's difficult even for yourself to know how you stand with a boyfriend or girlfriend. *Going steady* used to describe two teenagers who were somewhat committed to each other; now, *We're goin' out* can mean anything from *We're just friends* to *We'll be engaged in a month*.

Though the terminology has changed, boyfriends and girlfriends still tend to narrow their friendships down to include only each other. And this way of relating causes the same problems it always has.

"But What's So Wrong With Going Out?"

Let's say you decide with your boyfriend or girlfriend that you're both committed enough to be going out. That decision usually includes a silent but understood agreement that each of you will not date anyone else.

This exclusive right to the other person can imply much more than simply *who* one can date. Most young couples assume with this agreement that the partner is now the personal property of the other — that is, if you're going out or dating, you'd better be together constantly or have a doggone good reason why you aren't. A few mature and courageous couples buck this unspoken rule; but most abide by it faithfully. They may not even enjoy this aspect of dating, but they do it anyway because they're too insecure to do anything about it.

What is "too much" time together? Here's one way to find out: ask yourself if you're still doing the things you did before you started dating, and if you're spending time with friends you had before you started dating. In other words, does your relationship permit you and your partner to have separate friends and different interests? Healthy relationships—especially the Agape, for-you kind—aren't satisfied with dropping everything for just a steady date. In the best marriages, husbands and wives make and keep close friends outside their marriages. Why should dating be any different?

"I Can't Breathe!"

If you abide by the great American dating rule of dropping everyone and everything else except each other, you'll eventually smother each other. You'll still feel strongly for your partner, but there'll soon be a hemmed-in feeling, an urge to run away in order to breathe. And if you sense that your partner wants to back off a little for a change of pace, your fear of losing him or her will likely cause you to cling tighter and demand even more, thus driving your boyfriend or girlfriend even farther away. You'll actually cause what you fear most.

Exclusive dating relationships inevitably produce at least one smothered partner, which results in the death of most friendships.

"What D'ya Want To Eat Lunch With Someone Else For?"

Whenever you fail to talk openly about what you expect from each other, you're inviting problems. If you expect your partner to spend his or her free time with you, and they don't, then you'll probably feel hurt—which may cause you to lash out at whoever or whatever "stole" your partner from you.

In other words, it may cause intense jealousy.

What To Do About Jealousy

First, talk with your partner about what you think is causing your hurt feelings. Then try to agree on how to alleviate those hurt feelings. You'll need to agree on how much time you'll spend together from now on, how much time you want to spend apart, with whom you want to spend your time, and so on. The more you get out in the open—and it may be painful—the less chance there'll be of misunderstandings and consequent jealousy.

If this sort of talking and reorganizing isn't possible or doesn't seem to work, you may have to simply and decisively back off from the relationship as much as it takes to lower its intensity. Then you'll have to try to figure out on your own whether or not there's a problem. Intense jealousy, for example, may camouflage a destructive need to control the other person. If this is the case, look out—your relationship may have some other trouble spots.

Backing off from a relationship is also a good way to discern whether it's characterized more by Eros or by Agape. Jealousy is an almost sure sign of an Eros relationship, and recognizing it in your friendship can help you do something about it.

Create-a-Date

Face it — the traditional dating schedule is stifling. Relationships break up because they get stale, because they get stuck in a rut of movies, parties, and TV. So give each other room — room for other friends, room for activities that only one of you enjoys. When you get together, spend your time together creatively.

Here are more suggestions:

• Maybe limit yourself to *one* night a weekend instead of both nights. (I can hear those screams from here.)

• Save the other night for a girls-only or a guys-only night.

• Take turns surprising each other with an occasional wild, new, and creative date. Just anticipating the surprise will excite both of you.

• Invite several couples to join you on some dates. A group date can be a lot of fun, as well as less tempting than the typical date. (Don't set yourselves up to get bored with each other — which is more likely the more you're alone together.)

• Invest some time and energy in planning and throwing a party for someone else — your youth worker, favorite teacher, or a parent.

• Do a service project together — like helping out at a convalescent hospital or rescue mission, or taking some neighborhood kids out for pizza and ice cream.

• Plan a few active dates — tennis instead of movies, or waterskiing instead of sunbathing. Learn something together, like golf or racquetball.

With some brainstorming, you'll enrich your relationship and be the envy of your school.

Sure, offering each other emotional and social space is rare these days — but your relationship will be stronger for it. You won't get sick of each other. You'll both be growing individually, so that when you come together you'll have the freshness of others in your lives which you can give as a gift to each other.

A folk proverb compares love to a bird held in your hand. Squeeze it too hard and you'll kill it. Loosen your grip too much and it may fly away and leave you. But if you open your hand and risk losing that which you love, and the bird stays — or if it flies away, and then returns . . . *that's* love.

In a word . . .

Too much time together ruins relationships by causing one or both partners to feel smothered or jealous. Give your loved one the room to be their own person.

Ask yourself—

1. Describe the average couple's amount of time together. What do think is the ideal amount of time a couple should spend together?
2. How can a relationship smother you? How do you start breathing again?
3. What is jealousy? How can you handle it?

CHAPTER 8

Sex: How Far Is Too Far?

"How far can we go and still be okay?"

That is without doubt the most-asked question I hear when I talk to kids about dating. What they usually mean is "We like each other—how much sex and physical intimacy can we enjoy without it affecting our relationship?"

That's a good question. To answer it, let's get into our time machine and go back a few years.

For most cultures in the past, it was young teens who got married—and who therefore enjoyed sexual pleasure at a young age. This was convenient in a way, for a young person's sexual drive begins to kick into high gear between 13 and 15 years old. Young people were matched with husbands or wives at just the right time, sexually speaking. For them, adolescence didn't include a difficult struggle with overwhelming sexual drives. And so premarital sex was a non-issue.

For several reasons (most of them good ones), modern culture has pushed adulthood—and marriage along with it—back 10 to 15 years. While a teenager's sexual drives are still on schedule, modern

society virtually forbids marriage until some time later.

What society *doesn't* forbid, however, is sex. Whenever. With whomever. Tina Turner sang it best in "What's Love Got To Do With It." For most people sexual activity is no longer limited to marriage or to a strong commitment. The last 30 years have openly and drastically changed sexual rules. Are you old enough to make decisions for yourself? Fine—it's now socially acceptable for you to have casual sex with anyone you choose, as often as you choose. And don't worry about your reputation—it's nothing anymore to have intercourse with someone you've dated only two or three times. Commitment and marriage are only incidentally connected. Sex is simply a fun pastime, like skiing or ping-pong, that even two strangers can enjoy (by mutual consent) without the puritanical pressures of morality and guilt.

Society's view of sex has changed, but God's has not. Despite how modern life has changed, God still says no to sexual intercourse outside the boundaries of marriage. This may seem unfair to you. "Is this God's idea of a joke," some complain, "putting inside us strong urges and desires, but forbidding us to fulfill them?"

The answer is no. Not at all. God's list of goals for the human race doesn't include making life tough for us. On the contrary, he wants the very best for us. He wants us to "save ourselves for marriage" not only because it's better and more rewarding in marriage (although those are good reasons), but because he loves us.

He Created It, After All

It's true—God is totally psyched about sex. When God made man, he instructed him to "be fruitful and multiply" (Gen. 1:28), and this instruction implies God's approval of ultimate physical intimacy. He wants us to enjoy sex. The Creator gave us the gift of exciting, fulfilling sex. The Bible tells us that when a man and woman commit their lives together, sex makes them "one flesh" (Gen. 2:24). As a man and woman commit themselves to a love that can be counted on and trusted, sex binds them together as one. In this context of love and care and trust, there's an emotional and spiritual dimension to sex that can never be attained or even understood in any other type of relationship.

Furthermore, sex is a picture of the powerful, intimate, and emotional relationship he desires with each of us. To lower God's idea of love and intimacy to a mere joyride or one-night stand is to rob yourself of the incredible beauty and majesty of God's gift to us.

To ever know and understand sex as God intended, then, we need to develop sexual restraint and self-control. And in a culture completely devoid of any sense of right or wrong, it may help to see why unconnected sex leaves a trail of pain and destruction in its path.

Here's what I mean. Let's say that a couple in high school feel sure that they are in love. They've committed themselves to the relationship and to each other, and they both agree that their relationship is strong enough to include sexual intercourse as a symbol of their love. With all these things in place, how could sex for them ever be wrong or harmful? It sounds so good, doesn't it? The right words are there—*in love, committed, both agree.* Only one factor remains to be considered: are they *absolutely certain* that their love is a lasting and committed relationship?

If so, the only proof of that to God, to the world, and to each other is a legal marriage. "But just a minute," some may say. "Marriage is only a piece of paper. What matters is what we know in our hearts." Yet our society has set up only one way of officially proclaiming a commitment to unity—and that is marriage.

Face it—even in the best teenage relationships intimate sexual activity will most likely ruin it. The reason is simple—sexual intimacy outside of a firm, trusting Agape commitment is selfish. When you're not absolutely committed to a relationship, then you don't want what is best for your partner. Without commitment you want merely something for yourself. Sometimes it's not even the physical pleasure that sex offers, but rather a reputation you want to keep or a need to control a person. (It's well known that men frequently use affection to get sex from and power over a woman, and that women frequently use sex to get affection from and control over a man.) I've known far too many who have been deeply wounded by selfishness and even sexual abuse—all in the name of a love relationship.

Sexual intimacy outside of a committed marriage is wrong relationally, emotionally, physically, and morally. And here's why I think so.

Fooled Into a False Intimacy

Uncommitted sexuality is dangerous, first of all, because sexual intimacy and passion can disguise themselves as love and give you a false sense of closeness in a relationship. "Sexuality mimics love," claims one writer. "It compels tenderness and embraces, it forces the lovers to hug one another, to allay one another's pain through the revelations of sexuality, as when true love is exchanged."[1]

The scary thing about a relationship in which sexual activity is the focus is the overwhelming feeling that committed love really does exist—whether it actually does or not.

And what follows a sex-centered relationship that felt so much like love? "Disappointments," the writer continues, "a bitter after-taste, mutual accusations or bleak loneliness, feelings of exploitation and defilement. Neither of the two gave true love but only expected to receive it; therefore, neither received it." Premature sexual intimacy and passion only clouds whatever Agape love might exist between two people. Sex can be a desperate and deceptive liar.

Emotional Insensitivity

When a couple becomes sexually involved, their entire relationship enters a new dimension. Yes, there's more closeness—yet it's not due to more love, trust, and support. Yes, there's excitement—but rarely is there joy. Yes, there's security in sexual involvement—but it's as dependable as the security an alcoholic gets from a drink. Yes, it may feel good—but it doesn't usually (especially at first) feel right. Guilt and disillusionment often follow uncommitted sexual encounters—clear warning signs of an unhealthy relationship.

"I never feel guilty after sex," I hear people say. "I always feel fine."

For people to say this honestly, they must be so active sexually that they've become insensitive to the feelings following uncommitted sexual encounters. The only reason a farmer doesn't have sore hands at the end of the day is because of the callouses he's developed during his decades of strenuous work. When he started, you can bet his hands hurt plenty. He can work a long day without pain now—but at what cost? He hasn't been able to feel his cat's soft coat now for years. Likewise, the emotional cost of heavy sexual activity apart from a committed marriage produces callousness of the heart. You won't feel much pain and guilt after a while, but neither will you be able to experience the soft and sensitive joys of two people sharing total trust and love.

Physical Consequences

The most obvious physical danger of uncommitted sex is venereal disease, which is now clearly epidemic. And AIDS. As of this writing, no cure for AIDS is known, so there's no hope of recovery. You get AIDS, you die. It's as simple as that. And except for blood transfusions, needles, and childbirth, about the only way to catch AIDS is by sexual contact. AIDS has become a wake-up call to the hard lesson that unrestrained, uncommitted sexual activity costs a great deal. For this reason alone it's smart to say no.

Though not usually dangerous, pregnancy—another physical consequence of uncommitted sex—is disastrous. No disaster, most say—you can escape an unwanted pregnancy (we rarely say "unwanted baby") by merely removing the problem. Abortion, that is.

But to be sexually active and then not be willing to

live with its natural consequences is incredibly selfish and irresponsible. The most common consequence of sex is the conception of a child. What a gift—but what a responsibility. And by "terminating the fetus" you are jumping out of the frying pan and into the fire.

If you have had an abortion or are thinking about one, talk about it with someone you trust. In the first case, you may need to deal with feelings of guilt; in the second, you may need to consider all the alternatives before you make a decision. As you move ahead, however, keep in mind that there are definite physical consequences of violating God's ideal for sex.

Moral Purity

Our culture has cut itself off from a place to turn for moral guidelines and advice. For the Christian, however, God's moral law is spelled out clearly in the Bible. Jesus sums it up in this one sentence: "Love each other as I have loved you" (John 15:12). By teaching us how to love each other, the Bible helps us to see how God views sexual intimacy.

Speaking through the great Christian apostle Paul, the Holy Spirit has this to say about sexual morality:

> *You will remember the instructions we gave you then in the name of the Lord Jesus. God's plan is to make you holy, and that means a clean cut with sexual immorality. Every one of you should learn to control his body, keeping it pure and treating it with respect, and never allowing it to fall victim to lust, as do pagans with no knowledge of God. You cannot break this rule without cheating and exploiting your fellow-men. Indeed God will punish all who do offend in this*

matter, as we have plainly told you and warned you.
(1 Thess. 4:2-6).

God's desire is to make each of us holy—clean, pure, and whole. That means, among other things, "a clean cut with sexual immorality." When Scripture talks about avoiding sexual immorality, it's not talking about avoiding just intercourse outside of a committed marriage, but it's warning us to avoid any sexual involvement where the degree of commitment doesn't measure up to the degree of intimacy. In other words, the Bible tells us that any sexual activity is immoral (and therefore wrong), not to mention destructive, when it goes unsupported by a committed relationship. According to this understanding of "sexual immorality," a goodnight kiss could conceivably be morally wrong, and thus destructive to the relationship. It all depends on the foundation of the relationship.

When Paul says that "God will punish all who do offend in this matter," he means at the very least that the Lord will allow the consequences of selfish and uncommitted sex to take their natural course. What the Creator is *not* doing is trying to spoil our fun. He's warning us of the awful results of not believing him when he tells us that he's created sex as a gift to be used only within the context of a committed relationship. He wants the best for us; and when we hurt and abuse each other through selfishness and lack of self-control, his heart aches for us.

To fulfill God's desire for healthy and moral sexual involvement, Paul gives us three guidelines in this same passage:

1. *Every one of you should learn to control his body.*
When your relationship is based on Agape for-you

love, self-control will characterize your relationship. God has given those who trust him the promise that he will "not . . . allow you to suffer any temptation beyond your powers of endurance. He will see to it that every temptation has its way out, so that it will be possible for you to bear it" (1 Cor. 10:13). Sexual self-control can take several forms. Maybe it means saying no to situations that simply beg for trouble — like late nights in the back seat of a car, for example. What self-control will always mean is open communication with your partner and helping each other stick to what is best.

2. *Our body is not "an instrument for self-gratification."* Contrary to the ads, life is not lived solely for pleasure and our bodies are not simply utensils for grabbing all the gusto you can get. Our bodies are sacred, holy temples — buildings undeniably connected to our hearts and minds. We're not spirits trapped in a shell, but creations of God — body, soul, and spirit. So many talk these days about their bodies as if they were separate things to be used for temporary pleasure. To the contrary, God's desire is that we see our bodies as an important part of who we are. A physical body is not just a tool.

3. *You cannot break this rule without in some way cheating and exploiting your fellow-man.* With these words Paul gives God's final answer to casual, recreational sex. Uncommitted sex, at any level of intimacy — whether kissing or intercourse — will destroy your partner. Sexual intimacy is far more powerful and far-reaching than the physical act of two connected bodies. The beauty of love is destroyed when sexual intimacy surpasses the degree of commitment and trust in a relationship.

The Only Safe Sex

Don't take sexual selfishness lightly. You are playing with fire when you scoff at God's design for physical intimacy. Trust him to help you to be self-controlled, to be careful in your sexual decision making. Here's how you can work at it:

• **Avoid tempting situations.** It's much harder to do what you know is right when you're in extremely tempting or compromising positions. Girls, watch what you wear. Guys, watch where you look.

• **Make decisions about sexual standards ahead of time.** It's easier making clear decisions *before* rather than *during* battle. The best way to avoid problems in the physical area is to set limits of physical intimacy *before* you face the temptation. If things get too heavy, take a walk together if you have to, or go to a restaurant and talk things out.

• **Be honest about feelings and impressions.** Don't hide from each other. If there's anything bothering you, it's far better to risk talking honestly about it than to guarantee pain down the road both for yourself and your partner. Be sensitive to your own feelings—listen to your spirit. Dealing with yourself openly and honestly will help set solid, healthy patterns.

• **Try to live with nothing to be ashamed of.** Here's one way to do this: until there's a serious commitment (like engagement), don't allow yourself to go any farther physically than you'd feel comfortable doing if your parents walked in. A fairly accurate indication of guilt is a feeling that you have something to hide and to be ashamed of.

Even if both of you desire heavy sexual involvement, that doesn't make it right. You're still subject to the same devastating consequences as everyone else. Even with mutual consent, uncommitted sexual involvement will bring pain and brokenness.

In a word . . .

Heavy sexual involvement outside of a committed marriage relationship is relationally, emotionally, physically, and morally unhealthy and wrong. The way to have a healthy physical relationship is to avoid selfishness and any activity that's not appropriate for the amount of commitment in the relationship.

Ask yourself—

1. When is sexual intimacy selfish? When is it not?
2. What is God's ideal for sex?
3. Why is self-control and restraint from heavy sexual involvement a good idea?
4. What steps can I take to avoid destroying my relationship with too much sexual involvement?

CHAPTER 9

Intimacy:
All Grown Up
and
No Place To Go

Steve was an outgoing, energetic high-school freshman—a great athlete, popular, lots of self-confidence.

Gina was pretty and well-known, one of those girls who seemed to always have a guy in tow and yet was constantly looking for another. When Steve met Gina, he fell for her—hard. He couldn't stop talking about her. That summer they started going out.

Their relationship started like most—heavily involved emotionally, socially, sexually. They were also growing intellectually intimate, sharing with each other their deepest secrets and fears.

In August Steve and I went with several of his buddies to a Young Life camp. During that week Steve decided that it was time to give his life to Christ. Because he wanted to hold nothing back in living for Christ, he told me all about Gina—how much he loved her, how tight they were, how deeply involved they were sexually—and he asked me for

some advice. Steve convinced me as we talked that he really cared for Gina and that he wanted the relationship to take a healthy turn. He agreed that for things to turn around they'd have to take a few steps backwards and cool off the intimacy of the relationship.

Steve sold this idea to Gina, for she, too, was interested in learning more about Christ. They backed off from their heavy sexual involvement and made some good decisions regarding their physical relationship. They felt that this sacrifice was all they needed to ease the intensity of their relationship. It was okay, they figured, to continue their intimacy as long as their physical relationship was pure, healthy, and aboveboard in God's eyes.

As the months went by, Steve and Gina continued to cling to each other. In their eyes, each was that "special someone" to the other—someone in whom they could completely confide. Together they were in heaven; apart they were lonely.

Almost a year into the relationship, however, Gina changed. She started to experiment with drugs and began to discard her friends one by one. Steve, who still loved her deeply, tried to ignore the changes. But Gina finally dropped him cold, telling him that she no longer loved him. Steve's heartache and pain crushed him.

The intensity of Steve's hurt was as bad as any divorce I've counselled families through. Strong enough to rule out suicide, Steve had still let it cross his mind. After all, he agonized, he had given his very life to Gina, told her everything, given her his heart—and she had walked away. He felt betrayed as much as hurt.

Their intimacy, although primarily emotional and intellectual, had caused him incredible heartache.

Intimacy Cuts Both Ways

"Communicating one's deepest nature" is how the dictionary defines intimacy. Every relationship has some degree of deep sharing or intimacy. How free we feel to open up and reveal our inner selves determines the degree of intimacy in a relationship. My hopes, my fears, my dreams, my failures, my view of myself, my view of others—these are all related to who I really am. The more I open up, the more intimate, the more connected I am to that other person.

How can this ever be unhealthy? Isn't the growth of any friendship based on opening up and sharing who you are deep inside? Aren't you supposed to be vulnerable and honest?

Of course you are. But if you're normal—like Steve and Gina—such a high level of intimacy with each other eventually surpasses the level of commitment that's there. It creeps up on you and begins to destroy the relationship. For a relationship to stay healthy, in other words, your depth of sharing—that is, your intimacy—must not exceed the degree of commitment that you've promised to each other.

Why Intimacy Can Hurt

I know this is a tough pill to swallow. It cuts against the grain of everything you've known about friendship. But if you think about it for a moment, you'll probably see why indiscriminate intimacy isn't the safest thing in the world. Have you ever had one of those friends who was so utterly open and vulnerable with you that after a while you deliberately walked out of your way—a long way—back to your locker just to avoid her? You didn't really dislike her—you just weren't up to committing as much to the relationship as she needed.

Few people have what it takes to be confidants to every one of their friends. That's the whole idea behind *best* friends, those you know are committed to you—and you to them—enough to be intimate with. You know they'll be around tomorrow; you've logged enough time and experiences together that you can trust them with your inner self.

Dating adds another twist. Friends don't break up—daters and lovers do. With everyone you date or fall in love with—except for that one you marry—you'll eventually break up. Which means that if you develop a deep intimacy with every dating partner, you'll be hurt—because pain and rejection and bitterness is what you get when an intimate relationship dissolves.

When you've fallen in love with someone, it's common to think, "Wow, I really love him. I feel so good around him. He cares for me. I want to share with him all those things I've wanted to tell someone all my life." And as the relationship grows, that trickle of intimacy becomes a flood. All you've locked up inside comes flowing out. Here, finally, is someone who loves you enough to listen. But when the day comes that he's no longer there, it feels like everything you've shared has been abused, stepped on, rejected. It's as if he's stolen a part of you that can never be recovered. As Steve found out, the despair and the sense of violation pierces deeply.

Your need for love, care, listening, and commitment are adult needs. And you reveal those needs in an adult way—freely, deeply, intimately. Though your relationship may seem forever, and though it feels so right to open up to each other—if you've overstepped the boundaries of trust in your relationship, you're essentially "all grown up with no place to go." Once intimacy exceeds your level of commitment to each other, there's no easy way out. The odds are that this overly developed intimacy will eventually drive one of you away.

Two Ways To Avoid Unhealthy Intimacy

First, take advantage of those relationships that never need to break up—your family and your close friends. With your dating partner, it will eventually come down to choosing between getting married or breaking up—and chances are you'll break up. If you have other people—family members or friends who love you, who are committed to you, and whom you trust—then you can go slow and easy when you date without feeling you *have* to become intimate.

Another way to avoid excessive intimacy is to make a deliberate choice to keep it from happening. Easier said than done, I know. But even if the love you feel *does* last, why not slow down and avoid risking the relationship's health? Dating should be fun. Why squeeze a healthy, growing, adventurous friendship into a burdensome, marriage-like mold. Don't let your need for intimacy manipulate your relationship. Instead, allow your friendship to develop naturally within the structure of a healthy dating relationship—and enjoy the process.

░░░░░░ *In a word . . .*

Intimacy is healthy in a relationship only when it's supported by a corresponding degree of commitment. If there's more intimacy than commitment, then the break-up—if and when it comes—will cause unnecessary pain and a sense of betrayal.

Ask yourself—

1. Define *intimacy*.
2. How can too much intimacy hurt a dating relationship?
3. How can one keep too much sharing, too much intimacy from entering a dating relationship?

CHAPTER 10

A Prescription for Change

Things come easy for some people. When couldn't Reggie Jackson smash a baseball, or Robert Redford act, or Alvin the Chipmunk sing? But for them and us it takes know-how and study and practice. The same is true with relationships. A few have no problem being sensitive, giving, and caring. The rest of us who want to be Agape lovers need a lot of help. Whether we're experienced Casanovas or fresh beginners at this strange thing called dating, whether we've had successful, lasting relationships or left a trail of bodies behind us—we all could stand to take what I call a "dating physical."

Mousercize versus Flabbiness

During the last few years America has become a health-conscious society. Yearly physicals, six-month dental checkups, and social health classes have become a part of everyday life. And not only are people more concerned about health in general, but they're surrounded now by health spas, health food, and healthy diets that fight that great enemy of mankind—flabbiness! From the Disney channel's "Mousercize" to the line of "Get in Shape, Girl!"

dolls, there's been an increased emphasis on building and maintaining healthy bodies.

It's too bad that this same emphasis hasn't been given to healthy relationships, or at least healthy dating. We get just about everything else in school—how to speak, how to act, how to play sports, how to read and write and count. You can learn how to avoid getting pregnant, and what to do about it if you didn't learn the lesson. There are classes on how to have "responsible" sex.

It makes no sense to talk about all of that without first discussing how to have a healthy relationship. None of those courses get at the heart of what every young person thinks about—the need to be liked and loved, and the powerful desire for intimacy. It is incredible to me that high schools and junior highs don't have entire classes devoted to teaching students how to care for people and to be the kind of friend everyone wants and needs. Where do you go to learn how to have good, solid, Agape, for-you relationships? How do you even begin to "Get Your Dating in Shape, Girl (or Guy)"? One way is to take a "dating physical." Here's how.

Desire To Have a Healthy Dating Relationship

The first thing to do is to admit that your relationship—*any* relationship—can use some help. Chances are, there's at least a few things between you and your partner that can be improved. A dating physical is useless to those who foolishly admit no weaknesses in their own relationships.

Second, just as it doesn't make any sense to go to a doctor if you have no desire to fix what he says needs fixing, so you've got to really want whatever improvements a dating physical might point out. If there's a problem, don't hedge about taking care of it. Use whatever you learn about you and your partner to improve your relationship.

So be honest and willing to confront the results head-on. This is really the key to respect: loving each other enough to be honest, gentle, and caring, even when it might mean some pain. It'll hurt more in the long run to hold back and not talk openly.

Taking the Dating Physical

On the next page is a chart that contrasts the differences we've discussed between a relationship that's based on Agape love and one based on Eros love.

Toward the chart's left side are characteristics of Agape; on the right, characteristics of Eros. Between them are scales from 1 to 10 (a 1 represents a totally Eros relationship; a 10, a pure, perfect Agape relationship). No relationship is purely Agape or purely Eros; relationships usually fall somewhere between the two.

To take this dating physical, think about the categories on the chart (a relationship's *foundation*, how much *trust* is present, how much *security*, etc.) as they apply to your own dating relationship. Then circle a number on the scale between 1 and 10. It might help you if you write out a short sentence for each category that describes your relationship in more specific terms.

Take this dating physical alone, or take it with your boyfriend or girlfriend—whatever's comfortable for you. If you can take this physical *with* your partner, that's a good sign for your relationship.

EROS *(Unhealthy)*											AGAPE *(Healthy)*
	Foundation										
Self-centered	1	2	3	4	5	6	7	8	9	10	Giving
	Level of trust										
Conditional	1	2	3	4	5	6	7	8	9	10	Committed
	Security										
Temporary	1	2	3	4	5	6	7	8	9	10	Lasting
	Self-esteem										
Needy	1	2	3	4	5	6	7	8	9	10	Confident
	Feelings										
Engulfing	1	2	3	4	5	6	7	8	9	10	Fun, yet cautious
	Time together										
Smothering	1	2	3	4	5	6	7	8	9	10	Freeing
	Sex										
Self-gratification	1	2	3	4	5	6	7	8	9	10	Expression of love
	Intimacy										
Controlling	1	2	3	4	5	6	7	8	9	10	Warm and caring

Evaluating the Results

Now it's time for a long, hard, critical look at the foundation and fabric of your relationship.

What's keeping the relationship going? Friendship? Heavy emotions? A need for belonging to someone? A longing for physical intimacy? The question you should ask yourself as you study your results is "Do we both really care about what is best for the other person, or are we more concerned about our own needs and desires?"

You can answer that question by skimming the dating physical. Is the overall relationship healthy or could it stand some changes? The overall feel of the relationship will become evident as you look at the numbers you circled, and you'll get a general though clear impression from the chart.

So much for skimming. Now let's get down to details and inspect its fabric, its inner workings. Look at the dating physical again and think through each category, one by one. How does your situation measure up? Too much intimacy and no place to go? An overemphasis on the mere feelings of love? Anybody feeling smothered? Spending too much time exclusively with each other? Ask yourself these questions and you'll get a clearer picture of your relationship—especially of what needs to change.

A Prescription for Change

Just knowing you have a problem is half of the cure. But the other half is no cakewalk, either. A doctor can tell you that you need more exercise and less pizza, but it always comes down to old-fashioned hard work if you really want to get healthy. It's all up to you. So here are some ways to improve an unhealthy relationship.

• **Be a student of yourself.** Look frankly in the mirror. Face your own fears and desires. Get to know yourself. And don't forget that you can discover as much from others as from yourself. Tap as many sources as you can. Invite the opinions of others. Ask them, "How do I come across? Do you think my dating relationship is the best thing for us? Is our relationship as healthy as we think it is?"

Asking for feedback from others can only help a relationship. Those you ask won't always be right, but what they say can still help you think more clearly. I know it's tough to be open enough to invite input, but it just plain makes sense to take others' opinions seriously if you are intent on making your relationship the best it can be. If you are reluctant to ask others to evaluate your friendships, ask yourself why. Are you afraid of what they'll say? Who knows—someone else's opinion may give you or your partner the strength to face something that's been lurking around inside one of you for a long time.

Whether a friend, parent, pastor, or teacher, others can help us recognize what we can't or won't see.

• **Communicate with your partner.** Whenever you sense something wrong with the health of your relationship, let it out. Say something. Problems don't just go away—they need to be talked out, worked through, resolved. It may be the most difficult, scariest thing you've ever done—but if you care for your partner, you'll bring it up.

• **Take clear and decisive steps.** Or even a drastic step, if the situation calls for it. Perhaps you both need to agree to only double-date for a while, or even to not be with each other during the night in order to cool down an overheated physical intimacy. Or perhaps you need one weekend night apart to keep from smothering each other. One couple might decide to spend more time talking about things and less time doing things. Yet another may need to spend less time talking and more time doing in order for their relationship to get on track.

• **Make a choice.** Either you work hard together at fixing whatever's unhealthy in your relationship, or you break up. There's no middle ground. It's a simple choice if you respect and care for your partner. It's no fantasy world out there. You might as well give up hoping that everything will just end up all right by itself. Without committed and decisive action, the only result of ignoring your own diagnosis will be a painful and bitter breakup down the road.

Sometimes, however, it's just impossible to agree with your partner about your relationship. Or your intimacy with each other has gotten so far out of hand that there's no turning back. If that is the case, the only solution may be to break up as neatly, cleanly, and quickly as possible.

If you're going to learn anything from taking a dating physical, you'll need to be bold and put it into practice. And it does take practice! If you're like me— one who wants everything to be great right now and has difficulty with a gradual process—then learning to have a healthy dating relationship will not be an easy task. Regardless, it will take misunderstanding after misunderstanding and failure after failure before you develop the ability to meet the needs of others rather than waiting for them to meet yours. Right things, valuable things take time. Don't let the slow going and frequent stumbling discourage you.

In Chapter 13 I'll give you another tool that allows you to examine your dating relationship in even greater detail.

In a word . . .

Every couple needs to periodically take some sort of dating physical to evaluate their relationship. Once you do and discover your problems, you need to take these steps:
• Be a student of yourself.
• Communicate with your partner.
• Take clear, decisive steps.
• Choose to go for it.

Ask yourself—

1. Should couples periodically evaluate their relationship? Why or why not? Do they?
2. What does it mean to be a student of yourself in a dating relationship? How important is it?
3. Why shouldn't a couple just ignore problems, hoping they'll go away?

CHAPTER 11

Breaking Up With Style

During their junior year of college, Gary and Linda started dating. Right from the start they were recognized as the ideal couple. They were leaders in Young Life, went to church together, prayed together. They shared the same friends and the same interests. They were rarely apart. They and everyone else were sure that marriage was inevitable.

A year and a half later, they were still very much in love and committed to each other—but a few problems had developed. They had gone together so long and had become so intimate that they were all grown up and no place to go. Their relationship became characterized by intense quarreling and painful struggling as well as by subsequent floods of renewed desire, longing, and commitment. Adding to the tension was the marriage of their best friends. Everyone—even Gary and Linda—knew that they would be next. It was just a matter of time.

There was only one problem: Gary was secretly unsure about the whole thing.

Wondering and Wavering

For more than a year Gary wrestled with a strong

suspicion that God wasn't real excited about their relationship. He vacillated inside: "What do I do? Break up now and risk losing the closest person I've ever known; or take my time, hoping things will improve—and hoping God will somehow ease my mind in the meantime?" Out of the blue one evening, Gary finally told Linda that they were through, that he was convinced that God had other plans for both of them.

Linda was devastated. She'd caught a glimpse or two during the past year of something wrong with Gary, but she'd never dreamed it was this serious. The hurt ran deep—not only because Gary simply broke up with her, but because he had kept to himself the process he was working through. But Gary claimed that he *had* kept her up to date with his struggle. She had simply refused to listen. Gary may have been right; sometimes it's hard to hear the truth when feelings are so deeply involved. Maybe Linda didn't really want to know. On the other hand, Gary was a private, hard-to-read person; and it was obvious that he could have been more honest and straightforward with Linda. The last thing Gary wanted to do was to hurt her—yet by keeping his doubts to himself, he had hurt her more.

Had they broken up right then and there—really made a clean cut of it—the healing and forgiveness probably would have come in a relatively short time. But Gary fell into one of those traps that wait for you when you're trying to break up an intimate relationship: he could not completely let go.

Shortly after the breakup, Gary called Linda just to say hello. Although he explained that he still cared about her and loved her only as a friend, all the old, familiar, warm feelings of earlier, happier times came rushing back.

Gary's call turned out to be a mistake. To Linda, it meant that Gary still loved and missed her and would soon return to her — despite his stated intent to put an end to their relationship. Gary, on the other hand, simply wanted to talk with someone he still liked a lot. But Linda was totally confused. Did he love her or not? If he still loved her, she decided, then he'd come back to her if she was patient and waited for him.

Thanks to that phone conversation, Linda never actually let Gary go. She started calling him. Then Gary called her. Then he gave her flowers for her birthday, and they spent an evening together around Christmas. Six months after their supposed breakup, they were both so confused they didn't know what to do. Gary said he still loved her, but didn't want to get back together. Linda kept clinging to the hope that Gary would come back to her. They couldn't be in the same room together without creating an atmosphere of tension and misunderstanding for everyone there. In short, their relationship had become one big mess.

Minimizing the Pain

Respect and honesty in relationships sometimes means making hard decisions. If you really love someone, you must be honest with him or her and honest with yourself. When you need to make a difficult decision regarding the future or direction of a relationship, you are only hurting everyone involved by not being strong, responsible, and decisive. Sometimes that will mean hurting the one you love, which can be very painful. But you need to realize that you will cause much more pain and heartache if you're not strong and definite.

Let's take another look at how Gary broke up with Linda and how he could have handled things differently. First, the girl he said he loved deserved more than an abrupt announcement—she deserved honesty throughout the process. Gary's keeping all his anxiety and his thoughts to himself made Linda a spectator, even a victim. Gary should have talked and prayed with her about their relationship—where it was, where it was headed. Then they could have worked on improving their relationship, or decided together to end it. At least Linda would have had some idea of what Gary was thinking.

Secondly, even with an unnecessarily abrupt and painful breakup, Gary could have made it much cleaner. Although it was unintentional, his constant contact with Linda kept her emotionally tied to him. As much as he loved her still, it was unfair for him to end the relationship without giving her the time and space to heal. She and Gary both needed room to grow away from each other—to become less dependent upon each other—before they could shift into a more casual friendship. Instead, his being a good friend too soon paralyzed them both in a painful and unresolved process.

There are worse ways to break up, of course—the most common being to just drop out of sight as if there was never anything to the relationship in the first place. You know the line—"I love him so much (though my love for him has changed) that I can't bear to see him get hurt." And so she disappears, hoping that he'll get the hint.

Do It Clean, Do It Right

But there are better ways to break up, too. Whether you're tired of some aspect of the relationship, or whether you still love the person but know it's just not right, or whether things have simply degenerated to the point that there's no alternative but to break up—you can still break up with style. Here's how:

• **Be honest and real** throughout your relationship, and especially as a decision to break up becomes clearer. Help your partner to see what is going on inside you so that you both can understand more clearly what's happening.

• **Pray together,** asking God for his peace and insight. Be willing to wait when he says wait and to move when he says move.

• **Get some advice** from older friends you both trust.

• **Mutually chart your relationship's direction.** Should you put it on hold for a few weeks to sort your thoughts out, or is this it? If you want a cooling-down period, make sure you set a date and a time to get back together in order to talk—and then leave each other alone during that period.

If you do decide to break up, will you ever get back together again? Be careful with this one. Make sure you're both hearing what the other is saying. So often one waits for the other to come around, never admitting that the relationship is over. If it's truly over, help each other see this and agree to move on.

• **Part as friends—but part.** Make the break when it needs to be made. Don't give mixed signals or fragments of hope. Give the wounded partner time and opportunity to be healed and move on. Calls and letters and gifts may seem loving, but they make it that much harder to let go. Is it too painful to see each other? Then decide to steer clear of each other for a few weeks. Even in the middle of heartbreak, try to view each other as friends who need to part—not as enemies who have hurt each other.

In a word . . .

Loving someone means you'll care for and respect them up to and beyond the time of breaking up. Communicate clearly what you're feeling, especially feelings that may lead to a breakup—and then be honest, clear, and up-front all the way.

Ask yourself—

1. What could Gary have done differently in breaking up with Linda in order to make it easier on her?
2. Why is it a good idea to include someone else in your struggle over our relationship instead of just deciding you want to break up and then informing your partner?
3. How can you break up with style?

CHAPTER 12

Forgiveness and Healing

When I was a senior in college, my girlfriend and I got engaged. We had been dating for over a year and could finally say "I love you" to each other and mean it. So getting married seemed the right thing to do. The only problem was that neither of us felt deep down inside that our relationship was right. It was only a matter of weeks before the wheels began coming off and we broke up.

To friends it looked like I was just plain getting dumped by Josi, that she was the one ending the relationship. I was never honest or discerning enough with myself to admit that I wanted out, too. Instead, I reacted as if the breakup had crushed me. And while I was truly hurt and lonely at the time, I remember my secret relief when she blew the whistle on our relationship.

But I wasn't about to admit it the night Josi cried in my car and said we couldn't go on. Though I, too, sensed we weren't right for each other, I hated hearing friends say, "Well, Chap, if getting married wasn't right for her, neither was it right for you." Josi let go and moved on. I couldn't. I wanted to resist and fight and claw to get her back. I wanted to cling to anger, resentment, bitterness and not let go of them. I

95

wanted to make Josi into a terrible, evil, no-good monster. I wanted to lash out and hurt her, though I knew it wouldn't make the pain go away.

What I needed to realize — but didn't at the time — is that even the most bitter and painful breakup can be a blessing in disguise.

An Agonizing Gift

As devastating as it may seem at the time, a breakup is actually a valuable gift from God. It's his way of letting you know there's someone down the road far better for you. If dating is a chance to get to know lots of different people, then it's a lot like a test drive — it's okay not to buy a car after driving around the block once or twice. If you're dating, it's okay not to marry the first, second, or even third person you date. It's wise to shop around.

But breaking up is hard to do. It's tough to see it in a positive way — that God has a better person waiting for you. Instead, you are more inclined to nurse incredible anger toward your ex-partner — and perhaps to point a finger at God as well. "I want what I want, and I want it NOW! Why can't I have this relationship now? I don't want to have to wait for another one."

When my young sons are hungry, they want food right then — no ifs, ands, or buts. Pronto. I tell them, "Your mom has fixed a great dinner, which you will get a half hour from now. If you have a snack, you won't enjoy what she's prepared for you." Do they understand? Of course not. They get bent out of shape and cry and carry on like they're facing slow starvation. They think they can't wait. Instead of saying, "Really? A great dinner, just for us? Gosh,

Mom, thanks!" they act as if we're out to get them. They are too impatient to wait for the better food that my wife has made for their dinner.

Likewise, we are often too impatient to confidently wait for the exquisite dinner God has made for us and will give us in his own time. All God is doing in a breakup is clearing the way for a future relationship that is impossible if you aren't willing to move on.

Self-pity or a New Perspective—Your Choice

In the midst of the pain and heartache of a relationship gone sour you need a new, different perspective of just what it is you are going through. Think about it. Isn't it healthier and easier to wait for that special someone God has for you than to wallow in the muck of self-pity, wondering why you got burned? Waiting 30 minutes for dinner when you want a cookie *now* can be hard, especially when you're hungry. But trusting Mom and Dad to feed you with something better makes the wait tolerable. Similarly, God wants us to trust Him so thoroughly that even in the thick of painful circumstances we can have a peace that keeps us going and gives us a positive outlook. Whenever we've been hurt or disappointed, all we need to do is ask him and he will give us his perspective of our hurts:

> *Don't worry over anything whatever; whenever you pray tell God every detail of your needs in thankful prayer, and the peace of God, which surpasses human understanding, will keep constant guard over your hearts and minds as they rest in Christ Jesus.* (Phil. 4:6,7)

Even when you've blown it and hurt people or hurt yourself, God is willing to forgive you. It makes no difference how bad you've been. Freedom from pain and bitterness and guilt comes when you realize that God likes you as you are and has freed you from every dumb thing you've ever done. The past has no power to trap you into feeling guilty or dirty unless you let it. If you love God and trust Jesus Christ, you're his and you're clean.

Here's what God says to us:

> *In face of all this, what is there left to say? If God is for us, who can be against us? He who did not grudge his own Son but gave him up for us all—can we not trust such a God to give us, with him, everything else that we can need?* (Rom. 8:31-32)

> *You can throw the whole weight of your anxieties upon him, for you are his personal concern.* (1 Pet. 5:7)

You can forgive your former boyfriend or girlfriend and move on with your life only if you believe that God can be trusted. It's so hard to be free again unless you can thank God for showing you that you still haven't found that special one he has waiting for you.

And If You Don't Forgive?

If you nurse your bitterness at being betrayed and stop short of forgiving one you've loved, you'll be hurting yourself in several ways:
• **Poor self-esteem and guilt.** When people hold on

to the hurt of a broken and painful relationship, they'll probably ask, "What did I do wrong?" As they think and rethink about their part in the breakup, they focus the failure on themselves. Then they become unsure about their self-worth. Before you know it, they're taking sides with their former partners—"They were probably right to dump me." Which brings them even lower, down to where their guilt and low self-esteem paralyzes them.

• **Lack of trust.** It's only natural to be gun shy after you've been burned. But without forgiving and letting go of your partner, your understandable reluctance to put yourself out on the line for a while can breed inside of you an ugly distrust of the next person who comes along. "Guys want only one thing, and then they're gone," an unforgiving person is likely to think. What that does to future friendships is obvious. When you've been hurt, and you're cultivating that hurt, unwilling to let it go—you'll have a hard time viewing life through that tangle of thorny underbrush.

• **Loneliness.** This is perhaps the most difficult thing to recover from after an intimate relationship breaks up. It takes time to get over the loss of a close companion. Without forgiveness, the task is virtually impossible. The void cannot be refilled until you're ready to forgive and move on.

• **Bitterness.** Without forgiving the one who hurt you, you'll join that group of individuals who always seem to be living beneath a dark cloud. An aura of sadness and bitterness seems to surround them. Life has beat them down. They've surrendered to hurt or failure or pain or suffering, and their bitterness has stopped them from even trying to move ahead.

Forgiving, however, frees you to date again with

Agape, for-you love. Refusing to forgive, on the other hand, will demolish future relationships.

Speaking of future relationships—how will you know when you meet that special someone who's just right for you? Some people have waited forever for that one-in-a-trillion guy or girl to come along, believing that God places some sort of marker above their heads—a cloud, maybe—that says, "Don't blow it! Here he is!"

Of course God has a lot to do with bringing people into a relationship that leads to marriage, as Jesus Himself said about those who marry: "They are no longer two separate people but one. No man therefore must separate what God has joined together" (Matt. 19:6). But the question is still there: if God joins people together, how can I know for sure who that one person is?

Here's how I see it: once you find someone you love and care for enough to commit your life to, someone who returns your love with that same commitment—and you end up getting married—then you can know for sure that this is the person God wanted for you. The purpose of dating is to spend time getting to know different people and discovering the kind of person you feel most compatible with. That's what God wants. And as you date, decide to fall in love, and eventually get married, he will reveal to you the special rightness of the person he has given to you.

In a word . . .

When you've been hurt, let go, forgive, and move on. If you don't forgive, what waits for you is guilt, lack of trust in others, loneliness, and bitterness. The key to forgiving is trusting that the future is secure because God is in control.

Ask yourself—

1. How can you be forgiven for mishandling past relationships?
2. What do you need to do in order to move on freely after a bitter breakup?
3. What are some results of not forgiving those who hurt us?

CHAPTER 13

Using the Relationship Graph

Agape—real for-you love—is wholly and completely a choice. It is not, as many believe, just a good feeling or an emotion. Agape is an act of the will. If you want to measure how much real love there is in a relationship, measure the commitment. Emotions, time together, and physical and intellectual intimacy are merely indicators that help to determine a relationship's health.

This concept of love isn't as radical as it sounds. Modern social science, the Bible, and common sense agree: love is a choice, not just a feeling. Sure, feelings are there and they're wonderful—but they cannot become the basis for a relationship. Real love is a decision.

In this chapter we'll look at what I call a relationship graph, a tool that can help you to make good decisions about your dating relationships. With the graph you can measure the level of intimacy in six areas of your present dating relationship—emotional, physical, social, intellectual, spiritual, and degree of commitment. The graph is easy to use and, like the dating physical in chapter 10, will help you to evaluate and improve any relationship you enter. I've used the graph successfully to help friends, dating couples, engaged couples, newly married couples, and even been-married-for-awhile couples.

Here's what it looks like:

	0%	100%
Emotional		
Physical		
Social		
Intellectual		
Spiritual		
Degree of Commitment		

On the left side of the graph are the various components of a relationship. Along the top is a scale from 0 percent to 100 percent that measures the intimacy in a category. For example, if a couple regularly spent about half their available free time together, you'd measure it this way:

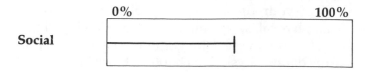

If, for this couple, the level of physical intimacy was merely hand-holding (each other's, that is), the graph would look like this:

Now if the first five categories — emotional down to spiritual — are like the mercury in a thermometer, then the last category — degree of commitment — serves as the thermometer's measuring marks and numbers. The two marks that divide that last category into approximate thirds represent two average degrees of commitment: the first mark — two 15-to-17-year-olds who are going out and believe they're in love; the second mark — a newly engaged couple. These two marks are arbitrary guidelines only and are dropped altogether once we start plotting a particular relationship. This will be explained in more detail later.

Before we plot the relationships of actual couples, let's define exactly what we'll be measuring in these six categories.

Emotions — Exciting but Unreliable

When palms sweat, nose drips, and stomach churns at just the thought of another individual, many think that these strange sensations mean they're in love. Such physical reactions, however, are actually symptoms of their emotional attachment to their beloved. So when they say, "I'm in love!" they're referring to strong feelings and the warmth of love they have for someone.

105

This emotional aspect of a relationship has a few peculiarities of its own:

First, this is the only aspect of a relationship that's involuntary. You can't control it by simple will power. Sure, you restrain yourself some, or pump yourself up a bit. But you can't fake emotion for any length of time. You don't readily adjust on the surface what you feel deep inside you. What's there will show itself.

Emotions are not only involuntary, but usually different for each one in the relationship. While the other four areas deal with something shared and therefore register the same "score" for both people in the relationship, emotions are rarely the same for both. While he's hopelessly lost in love, she's sulkily wondering where their love went. Her emotions are a tropical storm, excited and sunny one minute, and a torrent of tears the next. Meanwhile, he's like summer in Phoenix—110 degrees and holding.

No two people are emotionally alike—and though this may make relationships stormy now and then, it makes getting to know different people all the sweeter. It's the variety of emotions in different friends that makes dating an adventure, although a frustrating one at times.

Finally, emotions tend to obscure an honest assessment of the relationship. Strong feelings for someone, for example, can easily cloud the fact that this person is a poor choice for a dating partner. On the other hand, frequent fluctuation in emotions—commonly referred to as moodiness—can gradually ruin a deeply desired and otherwise healthy relationship.

Whether your emotions are steady or fluctuating, you need to acknowledge them and deal with them. For example, my wife Dee and I are deeply in love and are totally committed to each other. There have been days, however, when for whatever reason Dee's told me bluntly, "I don't like you very much right now." I know that her love for me and commitment to me hasn't diminished. As for me, I don't feel similarly about her. We just need to sit down, take some time to talk through whatever's bothering her, try to heal the root problem, and then simply wait out the storm of her feelings. Even during times like this when Dee's emotions are down, our love hasn't suffered — in fact, because we've taken the time to sit and talk and work things out, our love has actually grown.

Feelings — strictly temporary things — can hide from us the real joy of getting to know someone. Just remember to take them for what they are — indicators of wants, needs, and desires inside us and, secondly, outlets of emotional swings. Don't rely too much on them for any accurate measure of your love for someone.

Emotions, then, are generally involuntary; different from person to person, even for the two partners in a relationship, as well as variable within the same person; and unreliable for discerning the health of the relationship.

The Physical Side

Christian teenagers inevitably walk the razor's edge between wanting to follow God's direction in moral standards and, at the same time, wanting to get what physical pleasures they can from a dating relationship. A couple's sexual intimacy is graphed as it exists within the context of a relationship.

This is an important point, for many studies these days tackle sex as just sex, separate from the health and vitality of the entire relationship. The physical aspect of a relationship affects and is affected by every other aspect.

Socially Speaking

The amount of time that a couple spends together determines the score on the social graph. There's obviously a great deal of time that a couple cannot spend together—school, work, sleep, sports, and so on. The social aspect measures *free* time together, like walking to class, lunch breaks, after-school times, weekends, dating or studying, youth-group meetings, phone calls, writing and reading and endlessly rereading notes. Every relationship needs time in order to grow, and the social graph measures the time devoted to the relationship.

Intellectual Intimacy—Mind to Mind

After a talk on this subject, a girl asked me, "My boyfriend and I don't ever talk about intellectual stuff. All we talk about is sports and school and things he's interested in. Does that mean that we're messed up?"

Boy, had I blown it! I had to backtrack and tell her, no, the intellectual aspect of a relationship has little to do with how fancy or academic-sounding a conversation is. Instead, I told her, it represents the amount of talking and communicating a couple does. As it turned out with this girl and her boyfriend, I discovered that they did little communicating of any kind. They needed what most couples need—some plain old-fashioned talking about feelings, about fears, about hopes and dreams. Without this a couple will never really get to know each other.

Intellectual intimacy is closely related to simple friendship in a dating relationship. You may have butterflies when you're around your beloved, or a heated physical desire, or a strong romantic attraction—but without friendship to support it, the foundation of the relationship will be very weak. Friendship supported by good communication is the key to a solid, fun, and healthy relationship.

Spiritual Intimacy—The Inner Life

The spiritual aspect of a relationship may involve a particular set of religious beliefs (most likely if the couple are both Christians) or a general sharing of philosophical ideas. In any case, what's measured here is the inner life of a dating relationship. When a couple talks about their school day, that's intellectual; but when they talk about how God has changed their lives, that's spiritual.

Intimate, healthy relationships between Christians need a strong dose of spiritual connectedness. Prayer together, talking about and reading the Scriptures, listening to tapes, discussing points of spiritual application—all these help join a couple in an intimate relationship centered in Christ. The old adage is true—as two people deliberately draw closer to Jesus Christ, they'll find that they're drawing closer to each other as well. A great peace, love, and power waits for you in a relationship that focuses clearly on God and his Word.

Degree of Commitment

This is the standard against which all the previous

areas are measured. It is the foundation upon which the relationship stands. The degree of commitment (loyalty, caring, and love) is equal to the trust upon which the partners can rely. If a jilted partner laments, "But he said he loved me!" the degree of commitment was less than they both understood it to be.

You'll know how committed your partner is not necessarily by what he or she says, but by how he or she acts. Sweet, sincere words, even long letters of promises must be backed up with sacrificial, Agape, for-you love. Without deeds, words are merely convenient tools for getting what one wants. Sometimes, unfortunately, the actual level of commitment is revealed only when a confidence or promise has been broken.

Measuring the degree of commitment is pretty much a guess, of course. But one thing's for sure—the couple's degree of commitment is no higher than the lesser of the two partners' commitment. A chain, they say, is no stronger than its weakest link—and the same is true of a relationship.

Sue, for example, has cheated on Jim twice in the course of their dating relationship. He's forgiven her because he deeply cares for her and wants to keep trying to make it work. Lately, however, Sue has been avoiding Jim, and her commitment to him has been obviously and steeply tapering off. Sue's commitment to Jim, then, measures in at around 20, maybe 30 percent. Jim's commitment to Sue is closer to 50 percent. Their relationship's overall degree of commitment, therefore, is at Sue's level—only 20 or 30 percent, even though Jim's commitment is higher.

A graph like this one is admittedly open-ended, but the attempt to plot something as elusive and complex as a relationship is a big step towards discovering its health. And it will help answer difficult questions like these:

- What's the basis of this relationship?
- Is it balanced?
- Is this an Eros or an Agape relationship?
- Is there too much intimacy anywhere?
- Too little intimacy?
- How can we avoid the pain of a bitter breakup?

The next chapter charts some actual dating relationships.

CHAPTER 14

Meet Bill and Marsha

They met at a party on Saturday night. From across the crowded living room, Bill (a junior) and Marsha (a freshman) stole glances at each other. There was soon no doubt in Bill's mind that Marsha was as interested in him as he was in her. His glances became long, lingering stares. She returned his glances, smiling shyly, yet turning conspicuously away when Bill's eyes met hers. After what seemed to them an hour—but was actually 10 minutes—Bill grabbed a Near Beer and sidled up to Marsha and said, "What's your name?"

Marsha turned to him, Diet Coke in hand, and replied, "Marsha."

"Oh." Pause. "Do you go to Rolling Hills?" His high school.

"Yes."

"Oh." Pause. "Uh . . . good. Me too."

"Yeah, me too."

"I know—you just told me." They both giggled.

They stood for an awkward minute watching the dancers take control of the living room. Bill spoke.

"Do you like to dance?"

"Yes." Pause. "Do you?"

"Sometimes, but only with the right kind of girl." A

long pause. "Do you wanna dance?"

"Okay."

Both visibly relieved, they moved out into the room and began to bump, shake, rattle, and roll with the others. During the next few songs, Bill kept glancing at Marsha. She kept looking back at him. Both pretended they weren't looking when their eyes met. This game continued until, during the fifth song, they both decided to not look away. Their eyes locked. They smiled. That was it—the magic moment! The sparks flew, the violins played, their souls met!

"He's so cute!" thought Marsha.

"What a total fox!" sighed Bill.

The next song began—a long, slow dance. As Marsha stepped into Bill's arms, they responded to each other as if they were meant to be together. As their bodies gently touched, Marsha thought, "This is *so* nice! A boyfriend in my own school, and a *junior!*" She hugged him closer to let him know that she liked him.

At the same time Bill thought, "Alright! She must really like me. Man, I was thinking tonight would be a total drag. This chick's really goin' for it!" So he kissed her.

Long after that dance they are still together, dancing and kissing. Bill drove Marsha home afterwards and stayed at her house for a few hours.

The next day they went to the beach, but instead of sitting with other friends, Marsha and Bill spent all day together by themselves. They hardly spoke, but when Bill drove her home they sat in his car for a long time.

When Bill finally drove off, Marsha flung herself into the house and screamed, "I'm in love!"

"A junior *likes* me, Mom!" she shrieked. Her heart raced and her mind whirled. "He let me be with all his junior friends today. I have my first high-school boyfriend. I'll be able to meet all kinds of guys now!"

That night Bill and Marsha spent the evening studying together—mostly biology.

The next day Bill's friends pounced. "A freshman? Are you kidding me? She looks ten years old."

"I knew you were hard up, Bill, but . . . "

Bill wasn't sure what to think. On the weekend Marsha seemed okay, but on Monday she looked like any other freshman. He didn't want to lose the kissing and stuff—especially the "stuff"—so he tried to figure out how to look good with the guys and still keep Marsha on the side. He decided to avoid Marsha until lunch, but then take her out to a picnic lunch, just the two of them, to see if she was still willing to "have some fun."

So What Do They Have?

Let's stop here and take a closer look at the relationship Bill and Marsha have built since Saturday night. Using the graph, let's examine each category.

Emotion. Marsha is in love (sigh). Bill's not too excited about her.

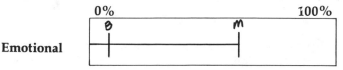

Physical. The first night they sat together on the couch in her house, Marsha pulled away from Bill's embrace and said, "I've got to tell you something. I'm a very moral person and I have strict standards.

Okay?"

"Okay," Bill replied. "I respect that."

After several hours of physical involvement, Bill finally found out what Marsha meant by "strict standards." By Monday, here's how far their physical intimacy had progressed:

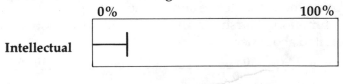

Social. Remember that this category is the amount of *free* time together. In this short relationship, Marsha and Bill have spent almost all their available free time together.

Intellectual. If you gave her three chances, Marsha could probably guess Bill's last name. He's pretty sure he could find her house again.

0%	100%
Intellectual	

Spiritual. He sneezed; she said, "God bless you."

0%	100%
Spiritual	

Degree of Commitment. Marsha is excited about

Bill because he's a junior and well known. If this relationship leads to other guys, that'd suit Marsha. Bill's realized that he wants Marsha only for private companionship and sex. If other girls come along who fit in better with his friends, he'd drop Marsha in a minute.

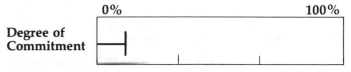

Now let's look at the whole graph of their relationship:

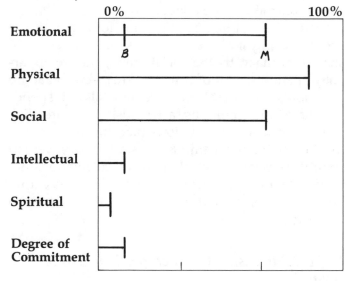

Is this relationship healthy? Most teenagers would admit it isn't. But why?

A brief look at the graph gives us one answer—the relationship is unbalanced. You could say it's top-heavy, since the top three areas almost exclusively control the relationship. In fact, the emotional, physical, and social aspects are almost all there is to the relationship. You can determine the healthiness of any relationship by looking at it's balance—or lack of balance—in the graph. It answers, among other things, the following questions:

What Controls the Relationship?

The thing to remember here is that the aspect with the greatest degree of shared intimacy tends to control the relationship. If two or three areas dominate the rest, then a closer look will reveal which is the actual controller of the relationship.

In Marsha and Bill's relationship, for example, the social and physical are fairly close in the degree of shared intimacy. By the social graph, they're apparently spending a lot of time together—but what are they doing with that time? Are they talking, spending their hours building a friendship, or are they playing with sex? It's obvious that, in this case, the heart of their relationship is physical. If they were to significantly trim back their physical relationship, they'd have to start over completely or break up—because other than the physical, they have no relationship.

Is the Relationship Characterized by Eros or Agape?

In other words, is there a stronger commitment to one's own needs or the needs of my partner? While the emotional, physical, and social are important in a relationship, they were not intended to be its focus. In healthy relationships, the emotional, physical, and social areas are the *results* or *byproducts* that occur when you cultivate the intellectual, spiritual, and commitment areas.

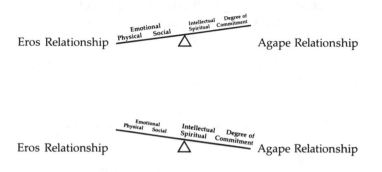

Eros Relationship   Agape Relationship

As two people share their lives intellectually and spiritually, forming some sort of committed bond with one another, their feelings go deeper than just friendship, or the emotional. They want to spend more time together. A desire to touch and be close grows with their commitment.

So how does this help us discern whether Eros or Agape characterizes a relationship? As long as the emotional, physical, and social aspects are *less* intimate than the intellectual, spiritual, and commitment aspects, the relationship is an Agape, a for-you relationship. It's a friendship first and a dating relationship second. Wherever any of the top three aspects exceed the degree of commitment, it is an Eros, for-me relationship. How would you describe Bill and Marsha's relationship—Agape or Eros?

Is There Enough Trust and Commitment To Support the Depth of Intimacy Between Them?

This final gauge of a relationship's health measures if there's enough commitment and, therefore, enough trust to safely back up and support the depth of shared intimacy. The graph makes the answer obvious.

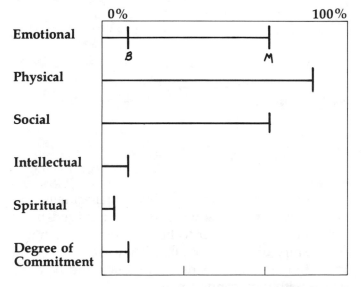

Although Marsha and Bill have been very intimate socially and physically, they have very little commitment or trust. It's clear they've not developed the trust to safeguard their intimacy.

"So what?" you say. "What's the problem with a couple being more intimate than committed? And what do you mean by *safeguarding* intimacy?"

What I mean is this: first, it's just a matter of time until one or both of them grows bored with the arrangement and they break up, for it's an Eros relationship, a for-me relationship. And the break-up will leave behind it a barrenness, an emptiness. For whether a couple's intimacy is physical, emotional, social, or intellectual, they give away to each other an irretrievable part of themselves. Intimacy is, after all, sharing with another one's most private, personal self—and if those I've shared my insides with decide to cut and run, they take a piece of me with them. The more of yourself you give, the more of yourself you stand to lose—and the more you lose, the more it hurts.

Safeguarding a relationship's intimacy, then, is to share only as much as the commitment backs up and supports. If there's little or no commitment behind your intimacy, then your intimacy is not safe for you. It's that simple. I can trust you to not use or hurt me only if I'm convinced you are committed to me. If you get nothing else out of this book and follow just this basic advice, you have a good chance of avoiding bitterness and brokenness in future relationships. You can be free to love only when you feel you are safe to love.

CHAPTER 15

A Look at Three Couples

Now let's graph three other actual, typical dating relationships.

Greg and Sheree

Greg and Sheree shot forward the minute I finished talking about relationships and intimacy in dating. Greg did the talking—and some shouting—for the couple.

"You have no right to say we're going to break up!" And without pausing for me to reply, he challenged just about every point I had communicated. Greg's reasoning was that their physical relationship—which was apparently heavy, though short of "going all the way"—drew them closer together. All that was (technically) forbidden them as Christians was intercourse, and they weren't messing with that. They were in love, he maintained, and enjoyed spending every free minute together. Greg did concede, however, that they were a long way from marriage.

After much coaxing, I finally persuaded Greg and Sheree to plot their relationship on the graph:

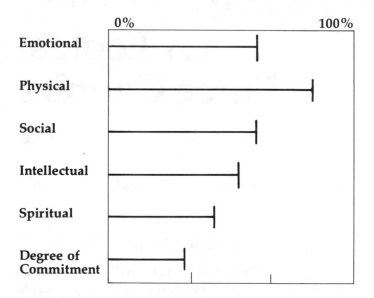

If they were seriously engaged and in their 20s or older, I would have advised them to back off a little in their physical intimacy, but I'd still call it a pretty healthy relationship. The problem was that Greg was 16 and Sheree was 15. Even so, their relatively low rating in the commitment area proved to Greg (and, I suppose, to Sheree, who stood mute behind him and nodded) that the graph was a joke and that it said nothing about their relationship. In fact, Greg concluded, they had a wonderful and healthy relationship. Sheree nodded.

What they in fact had was something close to marriage in intimacy, and yet shallow and fleeting in commitment. They were playing married. You know the type—they're together constantly, they talk and talk, they fight, they break up, they celebrate anniversaries. Sex is often the number-one private activity—

they save talking for the phone. And for a time it feels so right. But it doesn't take long for the romantic fantasy to explode.

No matter how right this type of relationship may seem, it will sooner or later show its true colors. The heavy sexual activity and constant togetherness that seemed so fun soon grows boring and stifling. If a deep level of trust and commitment doesn't control a relationship, Eros grows stale and old. That's when the real agony begins—lying, hiding, cheating, se ductive making up, more boredom, more lying—until the whole thing painfully and devastatingly unravels.

Sheree dumped Greg two months later. She told him that she still loved him, but that her love for him had changed—besides, she said, she wanted to date other guys. Translation: "I'm bored with you, so I'm moving on." An Agape relationship? Hardly. It was a short, exciting, selfish, Eros fling that left Greg bitter and broken for more than a year.

Donn and Christie

Since they sat next to each other in geometry, Donn and Christie soon struck up a friendship. At a school dance Donn asked Christie for a date the next weekend.

Within a month they had grown to really like each other—they dated once a week or so, talked on the phone every three or four days, and attended Young Life Club together, afterwards discussing what was said about Jesus Christ. (Neither of them went to church, but they were seriously considering becoming Christians.) They didn't spend a lot of time with each other out of school because they still carried on strong friendships with others. Sex hadn't been much of an issue since Christie's parents stay up late and the back seat of Donn's car needs reupholstering. Here's their graph:

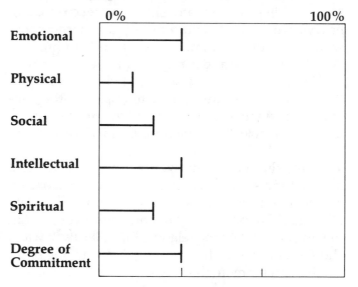

Four months later I sat alone with Donn and asked him about Christie. Everything had gone haywire, he told me. Christie wasn't sure of her own feelings since they bounced around a lot, and he felt smothered. As we talked I saw how much their relationship had changed. A healthy relationship that made both of them happy and content had turned into a complicated mess that ruined almost every day for them.

What Happened?

After the first few weeks, they had decided that they were now officially going out. It was this new status that changed things, that set up a web of unspoken yet clearly defined rules regulating their relationship. Donn explained that once you're going out with someone (what we used to call "going steady"), you were expected to be together most all the time—breaks between classes, most afternoons, every weekend night, even calls just to say goodnight.

So now, confident that they liked each other and armed with expectations, they did a lot more kissing. Not looking for a quick and heavy sexual relationship, they just did some heavy kissing. At first. "You know how it happens . . . " he said. Donn let his hands wander a bit. Then he had the back seat of his car reupholstered. Then special occasions took over:

Physical Involvement

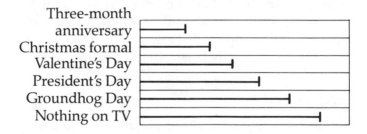

They stopped talking, because when they were together they were either fighting (because Christie's feelings were so fickle) or making out. Donn felt stuck and frustrated, but—because Christie still had a hold on him—he felt like he needed Christie. And she wasn't sure from one day to the next what she wanted.

To see how things had changed for them, look at their one-month and five-month graphs:

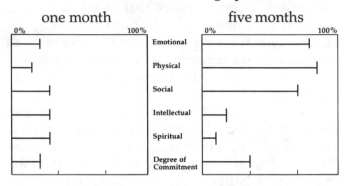

What had happened, of course, was that their Agape had turned into Eros. At one month their for-you relationship consisted of caring, communication, and commitment. By five months it had become a for-me relationship and was dictated by a heavy emphasis on sex and way too much time spent together—hence the smothered feeling that Donn felt. How had this happened? How could something so good turn so painfully frustrating?

Creeping Selfishness

Selfishness creeps into the picture when a couple focuses on what was before only a byproduct of their relationship. The physical aspect of an Agape friendship is undeniable, even good and exciting—but even such good byproducts, when they are elevated beyond their rightful, secondary place, turn nasty. It sneaks up on a couple. Rarely does anyone consciously enter a relationship for selfish reasons, but with time selfishness can gradually replace both partners' Agape.

Sometimes a guy's sexual drive deceives him into this substitution, and he thinks his physical desire is somehow a need that requires satisfaction — even at the expense of moving Agape out of the relationship's heart. His girlfriend, meanwhile, may fear losing the security she has in him and so gives him more of herself than she wants to in order to keep him interested and affectionate. Thus what was once a solid, healthy, and caring haven has becomes a smoldering battlefield. And it gets this way not because couples plan it (they just want to have fun and satisfy their needs), but because of their own subtle selfishness.

The simple irony is this — once you take your eyes off your partner's needs and desires and begin to focus on your own wants, you lose the ability to fully and freely give to your partner. If a relationship is healthy — that is, based on committed love, mutual trust, and good communication — you can know that your beloved will devote himself or herself to meet your needs and desires, as far as he or she is committed to you. You must trust each other enough so that, instead of worrying about whether you're loved or not, you are free only to love.

The Bible tells us the same thing in other words — "Think of Christ Jesus" (Heb. 3:1). If you take your eyes off Christ, then they have only one place to go — yourself. If you lose your trust in God that he does love you and that he has promised to fill all your needs, then in creeps selfishness. You become more important than your relationship with Christ. But Jesus Christ doesn't allow you to use him selfishly. He is King, he is Lord, and he is worthy of your love, commitment, and trust. Focusing on yourself will destroy your relationship with a girlfriend or boyfriend as certainly as it will destroy your relationship with Jesus.

Salvaging Their Relationship

But Donn still really liked Christie, he said. "We just messed up, huh?" And he wanted to know if they could salvage a relationship that has slipped from Agape to Eros.

"Sure," I told him, "but it's not going to be easy." Donn and Christie had a few things to do:

• They needed to take a long step backwards in their physical relationship. They needed to work hard at setting limits and keeping each other in line, even to the point of asking friends to help them.

• They needed to give each other room for other friends and interests. High-school students especially need room and time for a variety of friendships, for their interests—music or sports or computers or jobs—and for just being quiet and alone. Both Donn and Christie needed space away from each other where they could be themselves.

• They needed to make their friendship and communication the basis of their relationship, rather than the arbitrary "rules of going out." To swim upstream against the current of campus pressure and friends' expectations is a tough assignment—but I reminded Donn that those pressures and expectations created the mess they were now in.

Christie and Donn had a long talk that night—and decided to give it a try. It wasn't easy, but soon they were back on track. A few months later they felt it was best to break up in order to explore other dating relationships. They both saw this coming and talked about it a lot. When it was finally decided, they kissed, hugged—and moved on. Three years later they were still close friends. What could have ended in bitterness began a lifelong friendship—with no regrets.

Scott and Kim

Scott and Kim met at church. Their high-school youth group was huge, so they both had lots of close friends. They never actually dated—they just became close friends who spent a lot of time together, talking about everything under the sun. Their relationship can be plotted like this.

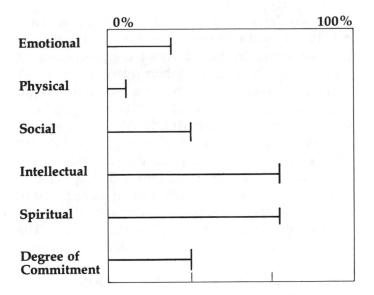

This is obviously not an Eros, for-me relationship. Yet despite the high level of intellectual and spiritual intimacy, it's not an especially healthy relationship. A dominant physical aspect is not the only thing that can harm a relationship. Even the intellectual and spiritual, if they exceed the degree of commitment between partners, can erode and destroy a friendship.

Here's why. In a relationship like this one, the degree of commitment is the most difficult to nail down. In a friendship commitment can be as high as 100 percent, just as it can be in a marriage. Good friends can be highly committed to one another, just as lovers can be. In either case, the nature of the commitment needs to be defined. There's obviously a lot of difference between the kind of commitment that exists between good friends and the kind shared in a marriage.

For Kim and Scott, that was the problem. They may have talked about everything under the sun, but they hadn't really talked about themselves—their feelings and the nature of their relationship. That's why their degree of commitment is low on the graph. They really hadn't discussed it with each other. Scott was looking for a girlfriend. All Kim wanted, however, was a close friend. They hoped for different results in their relationship. Scott's intimate sharing was a way of hooking Kim into a dating relationship—although he had never actually admitted it to himself. Meanwhile, Kim was happy with things just the way they were—she had her close friend. The trouble didn't emerge until Kim started dating someone else.

When Scott found out that Kim had a date, he felt angry, hurt, rejected, bitter, betrayed. Why? He had given away an intimate part of himself. He had laid bare his soul intellectually and spiritually—only, he felt, to be discarded. Although his broken heart was the result of simple miscommunication, it hurt no

less than if he had been actually betrayed. And although their intimacies were intimacies of the heart,
Scott hurt no less than if they had been sexually
intimate. He had trusted Kim with his private side
because he assumed that she wanted the same thing
from the relationship that he did.

When *any* area—emotional, physical, social, intellectual, even spiritual—exceeds the commitment,
you have the potential of pain in that relationship. If a
couple carries any aspect of their relationship deeper
than their communicated commitment to each other,
then, when the breakup comes—and it will come—
there will be lots of misunderstanding and hurt.

It all depends on commitment. A healthy relationship is grounded on it. And as your and your partner's hopes and expectations change, you need to
cultivate the habit of talking about them. Otherwise,
as Kim and Scott found out, there will be disappoint-
ment and pain.

CHAPTER 16

Your Turn!

The sample relationships in the previous two chapters have been fairly simple and easy to chart on the relationship graph. Not all relationships are that clear and so well defined. In reality the relationship graph will never be very precise, but it doesn't need to be. Its primary purpose is to help you to define the *foundation* of your relationship and the *fabric*, or inner workings, of it. All you want is a little clearer picture of your relationship.

To use the relationship graph, all you really need to know is the difference between the six areas on the graph. Make sure you know and understand all the parts and how they fit together. You should understand, for example, why the two degree-of-commitment lines (indicating "going out" and engagement) are placed where they are on the graph. Take the necessary time to make sure everything is clear to you, because the graph becomes easier to use the more it's understood. If you have any questions, just go back and skim chapters 13 and 14.

Once you have that down, you're ready to move ahead with the graph as a tool for you.

Determining the health of any relationship requires both graphing the relationship and then analyzing it. To accurately chart your relationship, the first thing to do—if possible—is to get together with your partner to work on the graph. It may be difficult for you and your boyfriend or girlfriend to agree to get together for something like this, but you need to give it your best shot. As you agree about where the various lines should be drawn on your graph, you can get a more objective feel for where the relationship stands. If you can't get your partner to join you in this process, take into account that your graph may or may not be a completely accurate picture of the relationship because it will be one-sided. Yet that may not matter much after all, because it is how *you* view the relationship that needs to be dealt with anyway.

So approach the graph with no preconceived ideas about the health of the relationship. Let the graph show you how the relationship is doing and let the conclusions come into play later. And don't conclude anything before the whole graph is charted out.

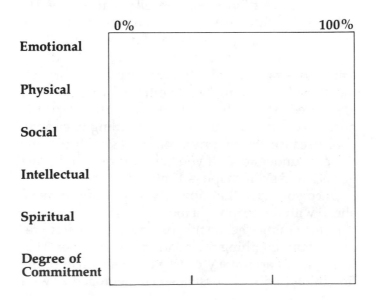

After the graphing comes the analysis. This is the time to start asking some hard questions. Just what is your relationship based on, anyway? You can usually tell when you see which category is the greatest. Is your relationship primarily an Eros, for-me love or an Agape, for-you love? Questions like these will help you to determine how much work the relationship needs in order to make it a healthy one.

Include in your analysis how each category relates to the others. Is there one area that dominates the others? Is there an area which has been neglected and needs to be concentrated on? What area should be reduced? Maybe deep inside yourself you've felt a little smothered, but haven't admitted it. Compare that feeling with what the graph tells you. Using both the graph and listening to those quiet voices inside, you'll arrive at helpful conclusions about your relationship.

Share Your Results

Now that you have completed the graph, share the results with your dating partner first and then with a trusted friend. See how others' opinions line up with your own conclusions. Opening up your relationship to the eyes of those who love and care for you can only help. With this input you and your partner should have some solid ground on which to build a healthy and rewarding relationship.

My prayer for you is that, as you give the graph a try, the God of all comfort and the Father of compassion will help you be an Agape lover. May his peace and wisdom guide you as you care for others and develop healthy relationships with everyone you touch.

CHAPTER 17

Putting It All Together

Now it's time to look at the next time you fall in love.

One of the things I hope you've learned from this book is that a relationship lives or dies at the point of distinguishing between falling in love and choosing to love. If a couple enters a relationship swept away by overpowering romantic feelings, chances are those partners are more in love with their feelings than they are with the other person. Feelings are a fun, exciting byproduct of a healthy relationship — but as a relationship's foundation, they're deadly because they are focused on oneself instead of the other person.

"Love Will Keep Us Together" — Or Will It?

An exciting reward of youth ministry for me is to perform weddings. Before I marry a couple, however, I insist that the couple come in and discuss their future with me before I agree to marry them. The first question I ask is, "Why do you want to get married?"

"Because — we're in love," is the standard comeback.

"Why else?"

They'll stumble and mumble about knowing that the person is the right one for them—then with renewed fervor declare that they really and truly love each other.

So I just keep bringing them back for counseling until I find out for myself one simple thing: are they in love because they've fallen in love? Or have they counted the cost of what a committed love relationship really means and have then decided to love this person for the rest of their life?

It probably won't surprise you that most couples decide to marry too hastily, without actually thinking through what they're promising to each other. A few have the strength to ask hard questions of themselves, of each other, and of friends they love and trust—but the overwhelming percentage of people believe that strong romantic feelings are the only thing required to make a marriage last. Whether couples have strong church backgrounds or no religious leanings at all, and whether or not they've heard the grim statistics that predict failure for half of America's marriages—still, they think they are different. Their romantic love, they believe, will certainly be strong enough to carry them through.

It's hard for a couple in love and contemplating marriage to realize that nearly all divorced couples had also fallen in love at one time. They claimed later, of course, that—for whatever reason—they had fallen out of love. And therein lies the problem. If you believe that love is something you can fall into and out of, then you've totally missed the point of love. You don't just fall out of a lifelong commitment. Agape love doesn't allow you to merely walk away from someone you've promised to love "in sickness and in health."

Choosing to love someone, in the final analysis, has less to do with *falling* than with *jumping*. Once you've chosen to jump, you've made your decision. You now have the great joy and responsibility to live out what you've promised—not only to your loved one, but also to the world. Learning to live with the choices you make and making the best of them is what makes life worthwhile.

The Laboratory Called Dating

While a dating relationships can be fun and carefree, it's also a valuable opportunity for learning how to be a caring, honest, and an Agape-type lover. The more you understand about love and the more you develop a consistent ability for caring even when it's not easy, the better equipped you'll be when you marry. If you're willing to work hard at learning to control your feelings, if you'll keep a close eye on the level of intimacy so that it doesn't exceed your degree of commitment, and if you give your attention to the needs of your dating partner at least as much as to your own desires—then you'll be well on your way to making your marriage a lifetime filled with joy, peace, and love.

It's never too early or too late to treat those we like and love with the care and respect we've talked about in this book. If you're in seventh grade and you're willing to work hard at being a person who's honest and unselfish with those you like, you'll save yourself and those you date a lot of pain. If you're in your twenties and have left behind you a trail of emotional corpses, go back and ask forgiveness where it's needed. Don't let the failures and disappointments of the past haunt you. Determine to keep yourself from falling in love without making a choice to walk in love. Wherever you are, now's the time to decide to be an Agape lover instead of a user of people.

One last word of encouragement—the commitments we make today are only as strong as the choices we make tomorrow. If you want to be unselfish in dating relationships and treat those around you with respect and honesty, then beware of allowing yourself to be swept into situations where it's too easy to make poor choices. Avoid overly romantic advances before there's a friendship, or telling little lies to avoid a confrontation, or letting physical intimacy get out of control—even once. Be one of those few people who chooses to love, and your relationships will be far more rewarding and fulfilling than you ever thought possible.

You have a friend who's ready and able to help you. When Jesus promised his disciples, "Remember, I am with you always, even to the end of the world" (Matt. 28:20), he was speaking to us as well. As you work at conquering the natural impulses of selfishness, don't go it alone. Jesus has called us his friends—but our part is to trust him and let him live within us. Once there, he's promised us his peace, joy, and power. As we grow in our care for people, he'll even do the bulk of the work—for the Bible assures us that "it is God who is at work within you, giving you the will and the power to achieve his purpose" (Phil. 2:13).

In a word . . .

Choosing a love and then being strong enough to live up to your commitment of love and care is the essence of Agape love. And we don't have to go it alone. Jesus Himself promised to be with us and give us the will and the power to love others.

Ask yourself—

1. What are some reasons to avoid "falling" in love?
2. Why should we learn how to choose a love?
3. How can God help us as we try to become better Agape lovers?

NOTES

Chapter 1

[1]New York: Viking Press, 1981, p. 87.

Chapter 3

[1]W.E. Vine, Merrill F. Unger, and William White, Jr., *An Expository Dictionary of Biblical Words* (Nashville: Thomas Nelson Publishers, 1984), p. 694.

[2]Vine, p. 693.

[3]Vine, p. 693.

Chapter 5

[1]Jane Norman and Myron Harris, *The Private Life of the American Teenager* (New York: Rawson Associates, 1981), reviewed in *Leadership* 3 (Summer 1982): 67.

Chapter 6

[1]Laguna Hills, California: Merit Books, 1984, p. 148.

Chapter 8

[1]Elisabeth Haich, *Sexual Energy and Yoga* (New York: ASI Publishers, 1975), p. 52, quoted in Dick Purnell, *Becoming a Friend and Lover* (San Bernardino, California: Here's Life Publishers, 1986), p. 55.